HOW I TURN JUNK INTO FUN & PROFIT

as told to Uncle Milton
by Sari

Remember: "It's not really junk. It's just something that needs an idea!" Example: An old hi-button shoe becomes a "camp" vase.

Published by

WILSHIRE BOOK COMPANY
12015 Sherman Road
No. Hollywood, California 91605
Telephone: (213) 875-1711

Library of Congress Catalog Card Number: 74-79533
ISBN 0-87980-278-2
Printed in the United States of America

COVER DESIGN / OSTER ZIVEN, LA, CA.
COVER PHOTOGRAPH / ALLEN ZIVEN

Printed by

HAL LEIGHTON PRINTING CO.
P. O. Box 1231
Beverly Hills, California 90213
Telephone: (213) 346-8500

INDEX

*"You <u>can</u> turn a sow's ear
into a silk purse"*

Sari *-1974*

Introduction
By Milton M. Levine

I first met Sari the summer of 1969. She came into my Hollywood office followed by three of the cutest little children I have yet to see. Sari told me that she had traveled from Chicago by way of Las Vegas and while she was parked in that glamour town her wallet, which she had left on the seat of her automobile, was stolen.

Here she was, an exceptionally good looking girl, with exceptional intelligence and with three exceptionally beautiful children . . . stranded in the big city of Los Angeles. It seems that she got here from Las Vegas with what little loose change that was left in her purse and with the use of gasoline credit cards which were fortunately in her purse rather than her wallet.

Anyhow, Sari showed me her book entitled "Junk Shopping With Sari," and I immediately became interested because even at that early date I knew that the United States would soon face a serious ecological crisis. I had realized that especially when I used to travel through some of the National Parks and see the junk which was disgustingly left at campsites and roadsites. I realized that the government would have to back up a tremendous campaign in order to "educate" the public to the distinct possibility of a serious ecological problem!

However, everything has its place and its time, and as good as Sari's book was and is, it was written just shortly before "its time." I understand that today the book is a complete sell-out and, as a matter of fact, is coming out in hard cover.

As with any product or any book—time is of the essence. So, I really believe that this book you are about to read "How I Turn Junk Into Fun & Profit" is both timely and informative. I believe that those of you who will take advantage of what you read will not only save a lot of dollars but will also make a lot of "sense" in both spellings of the word. Some of you may even go into the business of making things out of junk and selling them to appreciative neighbors and friends. Yes, I've known a few folks who have opened up shops to give instruction on making items out of junk and, of course, while they are quite creative people, I believe that Sari has inspired them.

I personally hope that this book will inspire you . . . .

A great deal of thought goes into the making of any product. I know that in my own business an idea may come to me personally or to someone else in the organization or that I might see something while driving a car or overhear something on the automobile radio. I immediately make notes in a notebook which I constantly carry on the front seat of the car, and the next morning about six of us here at the company have a brainstorming session. We thoroughly discuss the idea and each person brings up improvements or objections. 90% of the time the idea is kicked aside . . . the meeting is over . . . and we go about our regular business of earning our daily bread. But, it's that big, big 10% that counts! If the brain-storming session results in total agreement, the product is then put into the works and in as little as 30 days we have a product ready to present to our distributors. Of course, it's not as easy as all that and, as a matter of fact, some ideas are a year or two or even three in the making before they reach the public.

On the other hand, Sari, while she is full of unique ideas, thinks of something that she can do with junk and then goes out and finds the necessary parts and goes to work. If, for example, an idea strikes her in the morning, you can be sure that her "product" will be finished that evening. This is attested to by the reams and reams of papers in her voluminous scrapbooks and by the many, many samples she has on the homemade shelving in her home.

We are sure you would like to read about some of those ideas so Sari has had photos taken — incidentally, with a renovated camera — which are illustrated on the following pages. Also, there are some helpful hints and specific directions as to what to do with what and the type of materials that are suggested. If Sari has inspired you with the art of junk shopping, she also suggests that you let your imagination run wild.

Uncle Milton

I am absolutely thrilled to tell you that a large company, Uncle Milton Industries, Inc. recognized the many values offered to everyone of all ages through "Junkshopping." They not only asked me to write a book based on junkshopping, recycling, ecology and creativity. They even asked me to design a "Kit." Well the kit, Sari's Junk Box-Bottles and Cans, is absolutely practical, adorable and fun. It contains the instructions, secret tips and all materials needed to turn any bottle into a terrarium (You provide the bottle). Everything to transform tin cans into cannisters and containers. All that's needed to see that aluminum cans become candleholders and ashtrays. There's a set of plastic condiment holders that become the cutest photo coasters you've ever seen. Best of all, everything to turn any old shoe and a plastic detergent bottle into a beautiful, waterproof, hi-button shoe vase.

With a little ingenuity (and my secret formula) even damaged statues become exciting artifacts.

Introduction
"Sari—a Junkie"

Hi! I'm Sari, a "junkie"! Shocked? You needn't be. "Junkie" is short for "junkshopper," in my vocabulary. And, a "junkshopper" is a very creative person. Rich or poor, young or old, black or white, male or female, our "junkie" is addicted to seeking treasures at swap meets, antique shops, garage sales, or (s-h-h) even in dark alleys on garbage nights! These happy junk deviates invariably bring home an antique curiosity, a white elephant, or a beautiful piece of just plain junk. It's my pleasure, as the first official "junkie," to show you exciting and inexpensive ways to transform your treasures into lovely, one-of-a-kind furnishings, accessories for your wardrobe, or objects d' arte.

You see, I discovered "junkshopping" when I was a "budgeting bride" living in Chicago. The story goes like this . . .

To me a junkshop is an adventure in history, imagination and creativity.

Once upon a time, a young girl married a handsome man who didn't have much money by the time he bought her a big house. So, they decided to live furnitureless for awhile, rather than charge, or borrow, or steal. But, the young woman, anxious to sit upon a chair, wisely stepped into a junkshop one day. When she crossed the threshold, a magic spell fell upon her. All around were beautiful items, used, but at half the cost of new things. Though the young woman only had a few dollars "mad money," she conned the kindly old shopkeeper into selling her an old wooden chair, a tarnished candlestick, and a dusty, hi-button shoe. With her last dollar, she bought a tin of brown paste shoe polish, a bottle of ammonia, and a can of hair spray.

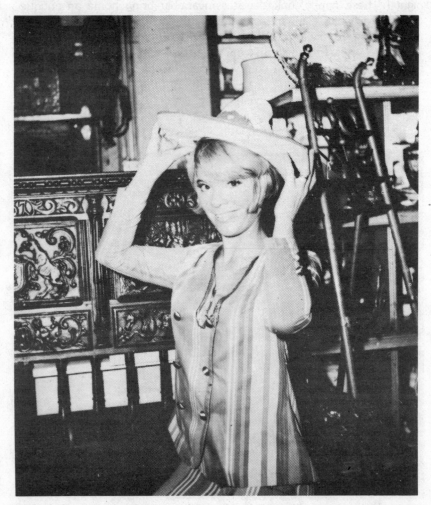

I've learned to recognize value in even the most humble items. Who says that an old hat can't become a planter, a serving dish, or a collage?

A few years ago, "Junkshopping" was a necessity for me.
Today it's a constant source of fun and adventure.
Bored or broke? Try "Junking"! You'll like it.

A magnet "tips" you on whether an item is metal, brass, copper, silver or gold!

My formula for renewing rust? Simply vinegar and water, and ammonia cleans brass or copper.

It's silly to pay almost nothing for an item, then spend a lot on cleaners, restorers and refinishers.

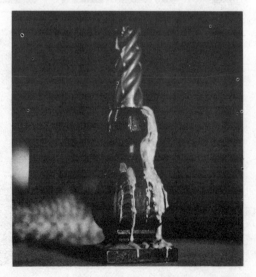

Later, as though touched by a magic wand, the humble chair glistened richly in its new coat of shoe polish varnish. And, it had taken only an hour to rub the shoe paste into the wood with steel wool! The young woman was pleased to discover that paste shoe polish is the cheapest, and the best furniture refinisher, for it's a stain and a sealer in one.

When the clever young woman held a magnet against the candlestick, it would not stick. Now she knew that, beneath the tarnish, there was either gold or silver, copper or brass. Presto! A little ammonia scrubbed on with a soap pad, and the tarnish went!

But, her secret delight, the hi-button shoe, became a real treasure when the young woman inserted a glass inside, added water, and arranged a bouquet of fresh flowers in this. As a last touch, she preserved the shoe's leather with hairspray. Which, everyone knows, is as good a clear shellac as any.

When her groom swept into their little palace that night, he praised her so richly that, hence, she was proud to be called a "junk queen."

Since then, this "junkie" has transformed "trash into treasures," coast to coast, for nearly six years. The whole world discovered my favorite hobby when a prominent publishing house asked me to write a paperback. Today, Grosset and Dunlap published "Junkshopping with Sari." My formulas, methods, ideas, and creations have been published in national magazines and newspapers such as Boy's Life, Woman's Day, and This Week. Also, The Chicago Sunday Tribune Magazine, and the Los Angeles Times Home Magazine.

The candleholders on my dining room buffet formerly bolted courtroom benches to the floor. They cost me 50¢ plus 5¢ for cleaning materials.

And, California has been good to me. For three healthy, thrill-packed years, I've endeavored to explore and report the western "junkshopping scene." I discovered that California, like Illinois, has thousands of "junkshoppers," and millions of "junk." All I had to do was put these two together! Voila! I knew I had accomplished this when my club bookings, and T.V. and radio interviews brought enthusiastic letters from thousands of fellow "junkies." Also, then a sophisticated women's college, Everywoman's Village, asked me to teach "Junkshopping."

My first T.V. and radio interviews brought me requests for programs on "junkshopping" from clubs and organizations. And, I couldn't believe it, the day W.F.L.D.-T.V. (Chicago) presented me with a contract for a "Sari the Junkshopper" daily television show. For one year, my little half-hour program brought an entertaining and inexpensive hobby to daytime T.V. viewers. Would you believe it! "Sari the Junkshopper" was nominated for an Emmy!

Soon, T.V. and club appearances might mean a flight to New York, San Francisco, or Los Angeles. It was inevitable—while guesting on the Ed Nelson Show, Ben Hunter, His and Hers, Tempo, Dialing for Dollars or The Dinah Shore Show—a sizzling love affair developed between Southern California and me. Today, I wouldn't trade all the Pacific sand in my shoes for citizenship anywhere in the world.

Today, as you can see, I've completed a new, meatier book—"HOW I TURN JUNK INTO FUN AND PROFIT." Naturally, this lively guide through antique, junk and thrift shops, garage and yard sales, and swap meets, is designed to help all homemakers have a "high-fashion" home on a modest budget.

My wonderful boss at W.F.L.D. T.V., Marcy Braun, even got hooked on "junking" as we planned the show.

Us "junkshoppers" would rather fight then switch.

There are chapters on where to find, and how to identify, antiques and other treasures. Tips on reliable methods I've used for refinishing furniture, staining glass, drying flowers, preserving trees and much, much more. Those seeking to express themselves through "art-decor" will enjoy the chapters on unique lamps, patchwork furnishings, soldering secrets, collages and off-beat candles.

Teachers, parents and children will appreciate the creative ideas for at home, at camp, or at school. An ecology-recycling theme threads constantly through "HOW I TURN JUNK INTO FUN AND PROFIT," particularly in the chapters on terrariums, macrames, hanging planters, rocks, shells and wood.

Have you ever cooked with pioneer utensils? Or, dreamed of finding and trying the genuine, original recipes of early America? I did. So, I gathered a collection of old cookbooks. Then, I tested the recipes on family and friends, updating and improving them as I went. The best of these including my prize-winning Pillsbury Bake-Off Recipe, are included in "HOW I TURN JUNK INTO FUN AND PROFIT."

Young men and women, especially, will appreciate the chapters on creating a unique, groovy wardrobe of coats, clothing and jewelry from thrift and junkshop trappings. All women will approve the cash savings from my antique recipes for making your own pure, simple, cosmetics and cleaning formulas.

Even more important, there are chapters on recycling those little things we all use daily, such as bottles, cans, tissue paper, material scraps, egg cartons, spools, newspapers, used aluminum foil, etc. You see, this is the "grass roots" junkshopping that's needed today. And, as you'll soon see, this is where I turned a good portion of my attention. Why don't you?

Old table legs transformed into elegant candleholders are just one way to recycle "priceless wood."

19

Chapter I
California or Bust
By Milton M. Levine

As you can see, an old tin mailbox is just as efficient and twice as pretty as a planter. Why not an umbrella stand?

Like all other dreamers who believe that California is the land of honey and the horn of plenty, and that Hollywood is the fulfillment of a dream . . . Sari told me that she had suddenly made up her mind during one of the cold windy Chicago days that she was going to make it to California or bust.

Of course, at that time she didn't dream that minor tragedies would happen to her over the 2,000 mile trip, and I am surmising that she was so enthralled with the lights of Las Vegas that laying her wallet on the seat of the car and leaving the car door unlocked was almost a natural thing to do. As I began to know Sari a little better, I learned that she was a trusting soul and, as a matter of fact, still is. Just get on the subject of making goodies out of junk and she'll give away "trade secrets" to any stranger who will take the time to listen to her.

Remembering again her first visit with me in my office, I can recall a dozen or more ideas she gave me for products. So you see, Sari is really a trusting soul, because I could have, although I didn't as yet, make any of the products without giving her a royalty.

At this point you might like to know that I manufacture toys and novelties, but aside from a product that I intend to produce using Sari's ideas for making stuff out of junk, all of my products are manufactured of virgin materials. As a matter of face, I have been producing a well-known item named the Ant Farm® and the Giant Ant Farm® for over 18 years, and I guess in a small way I am either famous, or perhaps infamous, just for having manufactured that particular product. Right now my Company, Uncle Milton Industries, Inc., of Culver City, California, manufactures well over 100 products in the toy, educational and pet fields. But, enough about me . . . .

Getting back to Sari, she told me that she arrived in Los Angeles completely broke and even a little bit broken hearted. She lost not only her money, which was her entire fortune, but a little of her confidence in humans and human nature. Fortunately, I am fairly well off financially, having been in the toy business for over a quarter of a century, so I wrote her a check, and I am happy to say that it wasn't a month later that she repaid it in full. She had almost forgotten that she had a big fat royalty check coming from "Junk Shopping With Sari." As I told you in the Introduction, she had written this lovely and informative book back in 1969, and while it wasn't exactly a best seller at the time, any and all royalties she received were more than welcome.

If you're as busy as I am, you'll be thrilled to learn that terrariums are easy to make, inexpensive and easy to care for.

Sari got hooked on junk and junk shopping when she was a kid in college. As a matter of fact, she sort of worked her way through college by renovating junk and selling it to other students. We'll hear more about this directly from Sari in later chapters of this book.

Sari was just a kid when she married. She told me that some marriages are built on cement foundations and some are built on sand castles and others are built on blue sky, but hers was built on rocks!

She didn't exactly tell me that her husband was "square" but he was just an ordinary Joe like most of us are and the word "junk" to him was exactly what it meant—junk is stuff to be thrown out on garbage day or perhaps given to the Salvation Army for a tax deduction. Sari's husband wasn't the richest man in the world . . . as a matter of fact, the only worldly goods they had after their wedding were the regular array of useful and useless gifts, and nobody remembered to give them C-A-S-H with which they could buy things to furnish their first apartment. As with other newly married couples, they moved into a furnished apartment smack in the center of Chicago. Those of us who have started married life in furnished apartments will certainly agree that the furniture and accessories in those units are not exactly what a new bride would wish for.

But, Sari remembered her college days and rooted out a $5 bill from her husband. Now, I'm not talking about 1930 when five bucks was fairly valuable compared to todays value of the dollar, but even then it wasn't enough to furnish or even accessorize an apartment. As a matter of fact, it wasn't enough for even a decent sort of down-payment, and Sari's husband didn't believe in buying merchandise on time.

Sooooooo—Sari decided to become an "interior decorator," but in a most novel way. Clutching the $5 bill close to her breast she wandered through the various department stores in Chicago's Loop district and went out the revolving doors completely disillusioned. "Now, what do I do," she grumbled to herself.

Then the thought struck her that what's one man's poison is another man's meat. In other words, why not shop the junk shops, or whatever they were called at that time, and maybe she would find something someone had discarded or sold for a very cheap price which she could buy and recover or refinish.

This was really the beginning of Sari's career and that career lasted through four children, two marriages, and here we are two books later.

That career has made her and is still making her a good living, and today Sari enjoys the pleasure of living in an eleven room house with a bedroom for each of her kids, four baths, a swimming pool and all of the other fancies that go with a Hollywood home.

However, there is not one stick of purchased furniture, furnishings or decorations in that beautiful home. Everything—and I mean everything— was originally J-U-N-K, and yet, hers is a home to be envied. As a matter of fact, it wasn't too long ago that the Sunday rotogravure section of the Los Angeles Times carried a four page full-color spread showing the interior of Sari's home.

But, let's get back to the "on the rocks" part of Sari's first marriage. If you will remember, she still had that $5 bill in her hand when she decided to start shopping for junk. For some reason, which she still can't explain, she spent the whole fortune on several good sized rocks. It appears to me—had I seen those rocks lying in the street, I would have kicked them aside and if they were on my front lawn I would have called the police to try to track down the person who had littered my lawn. But Sari has imagination as well as good practical ideas. However, Sari's husband didn't really appreciate her purchase, and in spite of the fact that she turned the rocks into delightful end tables and a cocktail table, weathered wood from the forest, Sari's husband was still unhappy.

Shortly afterward they moved to the suburbs of Chicago and there was a lot of grumbling about the cost of moving those heavy rocks.

Several years and three children later, they had not only rocks in the living room but converted junk all over the house, and in spite of the fact that it didn't cost much, and in spite of the fact that it was creative, and in spite of the fact that it was really beautiful—the marriage itself was "on the rocks."

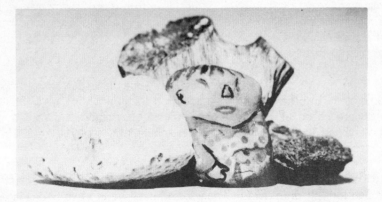

Rocks (and I don't mean diamonds) can become unique decorating accessories.

Chapter II

California
A Dream Come True
by Sari

When I went to the University of Colorado, in the Rockies, as a major in journalism, I never dreamed I'd end up minoring in geology. I already had one foot in the ocean from my many family trips to Florida. And, it was just as natural a step to want the other foot on a mountain. Geology offered me access to both, and that's probably why I decided to minor in it. There are few places in the United States that provide mountains and sea in a comfortable spot and where there's the kind of action that I also enjoy.

The most dynamic place, as many of us know, is still California. From college on I dreamed of living in the Golden State. Even after I married a charming geologist in Illinois, I kept this dream, incubating it yearly in my heart. He wouldn't leave Illinois; I wouldn't go without him. Years passed, children, a TV show, a lakeside retreat, a book, a new suburban home. What can I say? One day, for what I thought were good reasons, the children and I moved to Santa Monica.

Naturally, I chose to live on the beach. Ah, how the children loved it. We were literally counting the grains of sand for years. Believe me, when you've waited so long to have something, you appreciate it much more than those who just naturally inherit it. So, there we sat in a gorgeous, California-type, super-modern apartment, with absolutely nothing but our clothes. You see, I had sold everything, except the most precious antiques, even my silver, my china, my blankets and sheets. My giant auction had netted me quite a bit of cash, but now we had to start over. There was good reason for my sale—I discovered it costs a fortune to move to California from Illinois. I wanted to shed my old skin. It's my feeling that if you shed a skin you must grow a new one. I wanted to grow . . . and now I had the chance. I set out to find new junk shopping creations in a new California environment.

. . . Three Years Later
Uncle Milt Again!

As a bride, I enthusiastically filled our home with "beautiful junk." Today, I'm still doing the same.

I lost track of Sari for approximately three years, and by a strange coincidence I ran into her second husband, who was working in Santa Monica in, of all places, the plumbing department of a large store. He invited me to their home in Santa Monica, and I was pleased to see that they were living in a beautiful apartment building on a quiet street.

Sari had not changed at all, but, of course, the children had become a bit more mature and more beautiful. I was completely shocked, however, when I walked into the apartment, because it was like something I had never seen before. As Sari had told me she had done—although I had never seen it with my own eyes—the entire apartment was furnished with converted JUNK. She really knew the art of junk shopping.

Stretch your imagination a little while looking at the photographs on the following pages, and I'll have Sari explain room by room what she did and how she did it.

The farmer thought I was crazy when I offered him a dollar for his old chicken coop. Little did he realize that it would become a beautiful bookcase.

My antique china set ($15.00 in a thrift shop) is complimented by the preserved bread loaf filled with hollowed eggs and dried flowers.

Combined tastefully; antique brass, dried flowers, drugstore marble and an elegant mirror set a warm mood in our foyer.

A 400 pound fountain, purchased at auction, proves to be a lovely fish pond for the children.

It's a delightful paradox—an antique tractor and a modern gown and fur. As a model, I loved this picture and I have subtitled it: "Sari does her thing."

31

Chapter 3
A Home Full
of Beautiful Junk

A marvelous collage can be easily made from paper silhouettes or painted outlines of your family's hands or feet! Don't forget the family pet!

My first "hands" collage was a smashing success with my mom. An oak frame accentuates the bold orange and gold painting.

As I set out to "interior decorate" our apartment, I remembered that, about a day before, I had noticed thrift shops, the Bible Mission, and some fancy antique shops near the beach. When I went down in this area, I found the antique shops were quite expensive. It's a well-known fact that antiquing is becoming the number one hobby in America. And, "junk-shopping" is right behind!

At the Bible Mission, I met a lovely woman, Lucy, who said that she wanted to help me in any way she could. And, she really did! Lucy took me to a warehouse where there was bedding of all kinds. The mattresses had been sanitized by a large X-ray machine, according to California law. I ended-up purchasing three lovely brass and wood beds for a song . . . and they delivered them, too!

It was easy to clean the tarnished brass with a formula I had found in an antique cookbook—Pour pure strength household ammonia over the brass or copper; scour with a soap pad. I sprayed my brass beds with shellac (or hairspray) to prevent future tarnishing.

The best way to strip old wood, I soon discovered, is to brush on one of the new water soluble furniture strippers. To lift paint or varnish, let the stripper remain on the wood for approximately 25 minutes. Hose off, allow to dry, and refinish with stain and wax sealer. I always refinish my wood with paste shoe polish which acts as a stain and wax in one treatment. It's also inexpensive, easy to find, and if your furniture gets scratches at a later time, it's very easy to use for touch-up.

Now, everyone had a bed except mom and dad. We decided that we should try a waterbed at least once in our lives. So, first, we built a frame of long, barnsiding boards, cut, and hammered together. Naturally, we refinished them with paste shoe polish. Then, we put the waterbed inside, and filled it. It took me two weeks to make a bedspread of patchwork fur, suede and leather straps. I sewed them together, by hand, with heavy button thread. Believe me, my hands had blisters, but my bedspread was beautiful!

To effect the feeling of an entryway into the livingroom, I hung ropes of bottles, beads and corks, ceiling to floor as a roomdivider. We found the ropes, corks and bottles by the sea . . . in trash cans . . . at recycling centers . . . at junkyards. All were weathered, worn or very interesting. The bottles had one thing in common: They were various shades of green. None were identical in shape. First, we tied the heavy ropes to hooks, spaced six-inches apart, in the ceiling. Next, with heavy packing twine, we tied the bottles to the ropes, ceiling to floor, interspersing them with corks. The beads, in shades of green and brown, hung between the bottleropes, to soften the heavy lines. Our ecology-orientated room-divider was twice as beautiful when the sunlight bounced off those green bottles.

To me, a weathered, ornate daybed looked like good material for a livingroom couch. Believe me, it was a monstrosity, antique or not, when I bought it for $10. at a garage sale. Hammered securely together, stripped and refinished with paste shoe polish, upholstered with a fur-leather-suede patchwork, it was distinctive and charming.

One garbage night, as we nosed our car into the alley parking area, we saw a number of heavy, oak frames by the neighbor's garbage. Further investigation revealed eleven genuine icebox doors, minus the glass. Apparently they had come from either a butcher shop, grocery store, or restaurant. Whatever, they had been stored somewhere for a long time, to judge by the dust and rat's droppings adorning them. In minutes we had stored the icebox doors where the garbage man couldn't find them.

Another day, I scrubbed the frames with soap and water, and re-finished them with brown paste shoe polish. As time passed, the frames were extremely ingenious for holding mirrors, prints, oils, firecracker paintings, and a variety of collages. The two that hung above my lovely daybed-couch, were made with yarn, string and macrame materials.

You may use this technique on any frame, whether oval, square or oblong. Hammer small nails about 1 inch apart all the way around your frame. Now, lace the string, or whatever material you're using, to create patterns by wrapping it around the nails. Criss-cross, stripe, triangle—create any of a thousand patterns. I hung my two collages on chains attached to hooks in the ceiling. The effect was modern, airy, abstract.

Speaking of Firecracker Paintings . . . on dreary days, or on days when you feel you've had it from pressure, why don't you blow your mind with a Firecracker Painting? For this, you'll need a cheap canvas board, three tubes of oil paints in the colors you desire your painting to be, and three "lady finger" firecrackers. Go to a vacant lot, the woods, or anywhere where you won't disturb people, and lay your canvas on the ground. Squirt blobs of oil paints on top of it; place a firecracker, birthday candle fashion, in each blob. Light, and run! Pow, pow, pow !!!! Your painting creates it-self. Sometimes you'll get an ant or a piece of leaf in the oil, and that only adds to the charm. Be sure and sign your "original," for all the world to see.

When the sun shines through the green bottles and beads of my homemade room divider, they glow like jewels.

A 25¢ tavern sign, carefully reoutlined with oils, is truly a collector's dream.

An old straw hat, squashed flat, affords a unique background for a flower collage made from metal curtain tie-backs.

Chapter 4
The Heart of the Home
The Kitchen

My major concern in my new apartment, other than bedding, was cooking. Our modern kitchen, naturally, had built-in stove, oven, dishwasher and disposal. But . . . no refrigerator! I remembered that in the first lean months of my first marriage we had stored perishables out in the snow, until we could afford a refrigerator.

I was luckier this time. A new friend—a trusting, kind, dynamic, avante-garde gentleman, Milt Levine, (better known as Uncle Milt, or as the "ant farm genius") overheard my problem.

"Take the little fridge from the employee's kitchen," he urged.

And, he meant it. When I didn't take the adorable pint size refrigerator home, he had it delivered to our apartment the next day. I watched the mail for a bill, but none ever came. . . .

I guess I was the first, or one of the first, "interior decorator's" to "personalize" my refrigerator. I wanted it to match my black and burlap cabinets, so I sprayed it with black enamel. Next, I cut a burlap bag to fit to the door, glued it down, and let it dry. Meanwhile, I baked sugar cookies. When these were cool, I painted them with Tempera paints, and, later, sprayed them with plastic preservative. Glued to the burlap door, they added just the right touch of color.

As in most new apartments, all the walls were snow white. I decided to add color and interest in the kitchen with Primitive Kitchen Utensils. This collection is practical, for you can actually use your utensils for cooking, and it's fun to collect. Search for potato mashers, metal food choppers, crumber sets, old wooden spoons and forks, ladels, cherry pitters, etc. at swap meets, garage sales, antique and junk shops. You shouldn't have to spend much more than fifty cents or a dollar for each item.

I like to leave them natural, only with a thorough scrubbing, so I can use them in my second favorite hobby—cooking. For instance, I use my potato masher for crushing ice, garlic and potatoes. Or, if you should go on the warpath. . . .

Little did I realize that when my mother gave me a tiny food chopper, it would lead me to create a prize-winning recipe! As a matter of fact, one day a few years ago, I chopped some green pepper, some onion, some garlic, and sauteed it in butter. I threw in a can of tuna and some seedless green grapes (Are you nauseated?). Next, I baked a cream-puff recipe, adding a teaspoon of soy sauce to the batter. When the puffs had cooled, I served them, filled with the tuna mixture, as an hors d'oeurve at a Polynesian Party. Everyone loved it. So, I entered the recipe in the Pillsbury Bake-Off, which happens to be the biggest cooking contest in America. Also, the first contest that I had ever entered.

Several weeks later, I nearly had a miscarriage when the Pillsbury people called and said I was a national winner. They wanted to fly me to Beverly Hills, California, to stay at the Hilton for a week, and bake my little recipe with one hundred other national winners. Of course, the airlines wouldn't take me because I was eight and a half months pregnant with my son, Troy. I thought the dream had burst, until the marvelous Pillsbury people suggested that I take a train. They even sent a doctor along to accompany me!

I'm pleased to tell you that I had a marvelous time in California; I knew for certain that I eventually wanted to settle in the L.A. area. In addition, I won many marvelous prizes, and I made my national debut on television. Can you imagine how it feels to make your first national T.V. appearance, with a fifteen pound barrel in front of you, and mini-labor pains, to boot? But, I wouldn't have missed it for anything. And, incidentally, I did get back "east" just in time to deliver our son.

Now, I'm not saying that every man, woman or child that buys and uses primitive kitchen utensils is a possible cooking contest winner. But, I know of four or five who collected antique cookbooks, altered the unique recipes inside, entered contests, and won. It's even possible to change one ingredient and make a recipe yours, according to copyright laws. Why not try it? You can win up to $25,000.!

Most women like to collect crumber sets. Of course, these miniature dustpans and brooms are for sweeping the crumbs from the kitchen table, or cabinet. I thought mine was rather ordinary until I held a magnet against it. It's a fact: carry a magnet with you to swapmeet or antique shop, and if it does not stick to the metal you're thinking of buying, you'll know it's real brass, copper, gold or silver. If it does stick, you've got inexpensive metals or potmetal.

Now, I knew that I had brass or copper beneath that potmetal, so I stripped my crumber set with paint and varnish stripper. It worked!

There are many clever ways to display your primitive kitchen utensils. My favorite: Buy an old wood, or log, saw. Refinish it with shoe polish. Hang kitchen towels on the metal "teeth," or blade portion. Screw brass hooks across the wooden "handle" portion. Naturally, hang your kitchen utensils on these. This makes a unique addition to a rustic bathroom, for guest towels and washcloths, too.

One of my favorite "creations" is this weathered oak table-top transformed into a primitive kitchen utensil holder. Notice the "eagle" table legs and my Pillsbury Bake-off blue ribbon.

Primitive kitchen utensils are useful and attractive when displayed on an old school "cloakroom" hanger. Other three-dimensional "treasures" help contribute to a country kitchen mood.

Another useful, and cute junkshop idea for kitchen utensils, is to buy or find, mule, or horseshoes. It happens that army bases are throwing out mule shoes, so if you're near one, you're in luck. For fifty cents, you can have two horse, mule or pony shoes welded together. One should be flat against the wall, the other should curve out from the flat one, creating an upward-shaped "hook." These are also marvelous for holding shelving, kid's clothes, kitchen towels, door decorations, or . . . two horseshoes make a fantastic gunrack. Lastly, my husband, in an inspired moment, hung a muleshoe hook in the powder room to hold the toilet tissue. We both laughed at this expression of humor.

When I recall our cozy little apartment in Santa Monica, I remember how important each new addition was. We had started from scratch, and everything was important. For example: I found an old cutting board at a thrift shop for 25 cents. On the bottom side there were partitions that created the pattern of a setting sun, sending out diagonal rays. These supported the chopping-block top. It occurred to me that this pattern could be accentuated with various materials glued inside the elongated diagonals. Naturally, I turned to what is beautiful, inexpensive and natural — dried seeds, beans, and vegetables. I glued corn, kidney beans, and split peas into this picture. Later, using the same principal with all sizes of shadow boxes, I tried sunflower seeds, nuts, mini-pictures, mini-items related to nature, acorns, pinecones, etc. Shadow boxes offer no end to three-dimensional, doing-your-thing creativity. I still use my chopping block collage on T.V. shows, and in my performances, as an example of "how to create something out of nothing."

A 50¢ cutting board, bottom side up, makes a charming collage of dried beans and seeds. Remember: Beans and seeds are best glued with a mixture of equal parts—white glue and liquid starch.

Incidentally, it might occur to you to ask, "How do you hang a piece as heavy as a three-dimensional collage?"

Soon, you'll have to learn how to insert toggle bolts into walls and ceilings. Next, as I did, you'll have to learn the gentle art of macrameing twine and rope "hangers" for your creations. I did hang my cutting board collage in a macrame frame, simply because it would hold it securely, while adding an elegant touch of ecology.

If you like the idea of using nature's elements as artwork, you'll love what I did next. I suggest that you get a few old, interesting, uniquely shaped bottles. Gather seeds, corn, beans, anything that has substance. Drop into the bottle about one inch high of dried kidney beans, for example. Follow it with a half inch of corn, another inch of lima beans, etc. Filled to the top, these paperweights are very "in" for executive's offices, artistic kitchens, inexpensive, but elegant gifts. To look very "with it," just put a few around your home or apartment.

Though this hand-painted vase was chipped, I bought it at a garage sale and utilized it for storing potatoes and onions. Patch china with a little bit of chewing gum and oil paints.

Incidentally, I got so carried away with primitive kitchen utensils that I even hung my copper pot collection, my old lanterns and frying pans, and, as a matter of fact, everything that was interesting to me, from the ceiling of my kitchen. What better place to display my treasures? And, I could still use them!

The same is true for my scrub-boards. If you have never seen a genuine, used, refinished scrub-board turned into a modern, charming bulletin board, then you've got a treat in store. First, find the oldest, tin or metal scrub-board you can. These are available in the garbage, swapmeets, garage sales, etc. Make certain that a magnet will stick to the center portion.

Refinish all wood parts with only paste shoe polish. Glue an antique postcard in the little top portion, stick fruit or vegetable magnets to the metal portion, and screw brass hooks to the wooden base. What is it? Naturally, it's a bulletin board, key holder, collage wall-hanging all in one!

A valuable cigar mold, refinished with shoe polish, adorned with a brass eagle, is a perfect display for my antique spoon and fork collection.

Without a magnet, I'd never have known that the black metal on these lovely glass cannisters was solid copper. Household ammonia and a soap pad did the cleaning cheaply.

Old ice tongs make clever paper towel or toilet paper holders.

A pie-shell type picture frame, refinished with shoe polish, is the perfect foil for a red bandana collage with primitive kitchen utensils and my Pillsbury Bake-off ribbon.

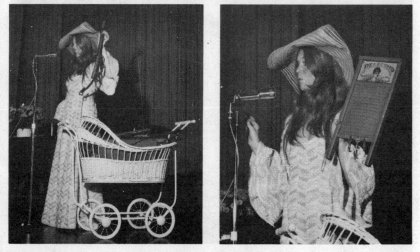

When I perform for women's clubs, I try to bring along about 20 of my favorite "Sari Originals." Among these are (left) a horse's harness that has been transformed into a towel rack, and a scrub board that is now a useful bulletin board.

47

Chapter 5

More! More! More!
Junkshopping Techniques

If you should happen to buy a 400 pound fountain at an auction, don't panic. With a little work almost anything can be transformed into a thing of beauty.

Thanks to an ugly, rusted breadbox, I chanced to find a totally new covering for wood, metal or anything. This breadbox was worth saving, to me, because of its giant size and nostalgic remembrances. So, I gathered scraps of material from around the house. I dipped them in liquid starch and smoothed them, one by one, onto the rusted tin. Like putting a jigsaw puzzle together, I watched my ugly duckling become a clean, modern utensil with antique distinctiveness. I lined the interior with aluminum foil, and put an assortment of bread inside. Now, that breadbox is a family heirloom.

Later, I used the patchwork technique on one of the first rocking horses ever made. Now, I'm not a garbage picker, but how can I help it if people throw away beautiful things? Shouldn't I rescue them from the trash heap? I think so. So I dragged this lovely wooden creation home, and went to work. Nose, ears, eyes, tail and hooves, I left bright, shiny red. The rest, I patchworked. Today, our little horse with its flat saddled back is a perfect telephone stand.

In another corner of our livingroom, between two old Bible Mission bamboo chairs, was a child's wheelbarrow. Sprayed red, patchworked and shellacked, this treasure is . . . ? You guessed it—a portable magazine rack!

I can see this idea utilized as a portable nut bowl, knitting kit, chess table. **Apply your imagination to items and personalize them to suit your lifestyle.**

When I discovered this pine chicken coop, it was covered with chicken feathers and . . . A thorough scrubbing, a refinishing with brown paste shoe polish, and it became one of the most attractive bookcases I've ever seen.

I'm certain that most of you have seen giant wire spools turned into tables. The only difference between my diningroom "spool table" and others was its rustic finish. I had beaten my table top with a chain, a hammer, and a nail. The children assisted me in further aging it to resemble expensive "wormwood" with fire. Lastly, we sealed it with a heavy coating of brown and black paste shoe polish.

Now, we needed chairs. Lucky me, I bought three barrels at a swapmeet for $3. Normally they sell for about $6 each. I also refinished these with shoe polish, after I'd painted a vine and leaf design around the bottom. I adore needlework, but haven't, as yet, had the time to learn crocheting. So, next best, I bought crocheted towels at a thrift shop and turned them into cushions for the barrel tops.

At the Saugus-Newhall swapmeet, where all the farmers bring in their genuine "goodies" on Sunday morning in Southern California, I found the answer to the three other stools for our dining area. All morning I had been browsing through horse's trappings, tractor seats, milk cans, chicken coops, etc. I noticed all the "decorator" items that are very expensive on Robertson Boulevard, had $2. price tags on in this small, farming community.

While rambling through the remains of an old building, I found the plaster brackets that support this lovely shelf. Hubby and I gathered the mugs at swap meets.

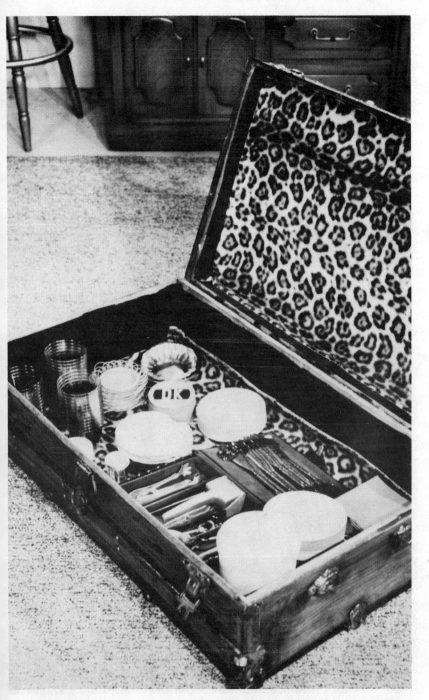

Trunks are very in right now. I've turned my foot locker into a coffee table, stereo cabinet or bar at different times.

I finally settled on three rusted milk cans and three tractor seats. Later, when the rust had been removed with a mixture of equal parts apple cider vinegar and water, and a good scouring, I paid a friend $1. to weld the tractor seats to the milk can tops. These made really clever stools. Sprayed bright red, I added stripes and designs with yellow and black decorator tape. They were really winners!

Thanks to my oldest daughter, Terra, we acquired a rustic fruit bowl large enough to compliment our huge spool diningtable. We were rubbling —a fancy name for garbage picking through buildings that are being torn down. Terra sighted a huge, rusted fire alarm bell. This half circle of iron had formerly been attached to the side of a building.

Somehow the two of us dragged that heavy monstrosity home. She spent the rest of the afternoon removing rust with a wire brush, a pail of vinegar and water and some scouring pads. Dad bolted the two pieces together in an hourglass shape. Spray-painted red, Terra's compote bowl was goregous. Believe me, with a family as large as ours, we need a fruitbowl that holds a dozen oranges, two dozen apples and three pineapples!

You can see that the lovely wood grain on this old trunk is accentuated by the shoe polish finish.

Serving as a buffet along a diningroom wall, I placed a large wrought iron Baker's rack. Because these are very popular in decorator's magazines right now, everyone wants to buy it. The truth is I wouldn't sell any of my "Sari Originals" for any price—unless I was tired of it, or had made a duplicate. However, I always give original "junkshop" gifts to everyone I care about.

It turned-out that I got this rack for the trouble of hauling it away. I'd sighted it behind a bakery. The baker said he wouldn't sell it—"It's trash. You can have it if you'll haul it away." It wasn't easy, but, somehow, I strapped it to the roof of my car and carted it home.

I remembered an old trick an interior decorator had taught me. To make metal look like genuine wrought iron, spray with flat black paint. While damp, sprinkle with sawdust. Allow to dry, and spray paint again. This technique transformed my rack into a thing of beauty.

From the remains of the old fireplace, a carved block can be recycled into an artistic bookend.

I had discovered terrariums. The little man at the glass recycling center told me I was his best customer. He saved all the beautiful, big wine bottles for my visits. As I mention in a later chapter, "How To Make Terrariums," there's nothing as marvelous as a lovely garden that requires absolutely no care. So, I arranged twelve or so terrariums on two shelves of my Baker's rack, and, what china and silver I had, on the others.

In a tiny alcove beneath the stairs, I created a "music center." The focal point here was a footlocker turned stereo cabinet. I'd paid $2. for that locker, but sometimes I see them by the garbage. Other times they sell for $6. or $8. Unfortunately, all foot lockers are covered with canvas. Believe it or not, beneath that ugly canvas there's gorgeous wood. Strip the canvas with paint and varnish lifter, or stripper, and some sharp scrapers . . . .

When all the canvas had been removed, the wood was stained with shoe polish, the brass fittings were scoured with ammonia, and the whole thing was sealed with plastic preservative. I lined the interior of the trunk with fake leopard, and added a few matching stripes on the top. Now, hubby installed the stereo. The sound was magnificent!

Slide a baby bottle into a hi-button shoe and you have the basis for a "camp" vase. Use a magnet and you might discover a genuine copper lamp or a classic statue.

Chapter 6
Imagination
Natural or Acquired

Over the years, I've met thousands of people who claim they have "no imagination." I always tell them: "Imagination is like sterling silver —the more you use it, the brighter it gets!" (Isn't that lovely? Well, at least it's original! And, it's true, too.)

I show them the "junkshopping game"—a casual exercise of mentally transforming various junkshop or swapmeet items into as many decorative or useful gifts or furnishings as they can think of. As the cobwebs slip away, they become more and more imaginative at "junkshopping." Chances are they're hooked for life on a challenging, inexpensive and rewarding hobby. I was. And, when my imagination had become keenly sharpened, I found a truly creative challenge in an odd, Tiffany-type lamp.

There it sat—a black, metal monstrosity that had long lost the beautiful glass from its shade. Casually, I pulled a tiny magnet from my purse. Unobtrusively, I held the magnet against the lamp. My geiger counter started ticking: The magnet would not stick to the metal! Now I knew that beneath all that black tarnish there was either genuine brass or copper. Apparently the shopkeeper was not aware of this; he had a $2. price tag on a much more valuable item.

For me, a poker face is nearly impossible. I managed one just long enough to make my purchase and get to the car. Then, I burst out giggling . . . until the doubts about how I was going to replace that Tiffany shade surfaced.

Real Tiffany glass was absolutely out. Not only was it nearly impossible to find, but it was far too expensive. Stained glass might be a little cheaper. But, would the old glass crack when cut to fit the semi-triangular sides of the shade? If I used plain window glass, the glare of the naked bulb would be garish. Believe me, I had a challenge!

First, though, the tarnish had to be removed. From an antique cookbook, I had long ago learned that pure strength household ammonia is the cheapest tarnish remover for brass and copper. Coupled with a soap pad scrubbing, it's also the most rapid and the most effective. Zap! Suddenly I had a shiny, copper lamp! . . . minus the all important glass shade.

Later, while shopping in a pet store, I noticed a product for staining the glass of aquariums. A liquid plastic in about fifteen colors, you simply brushed it on glass, and it dried, forming crystals and patterns. Most important, the stain could be removed with vinegar.

My imagination clicked: This was the answer! I had window glass cut the proper size. I stained it with a rainbow of colors, and fastened it where the real Tiffany used to be. Now, I purchased a large kerosene-type lightbulb. These can be found in most hardware and lamp shops.

Totaling up my expenditures—lamp, $2.; liquid plastic stain, $1.; window glass, $3.; and lightbulb, $2.—I had quite a treasure for $8. Though I may not be able to name drop about my real Tiffany lamp, I constantly receive compliments on my "beautiful monstrosity."

Would you believe that I retrieved this old cabinet from the garbage? And . . . it turned out to be a genuine French telephone cabinet.

Chapter 7
Garbage Picking
by the Light of the Silvery Moon

Now, I'm not a junkwoman . . . but, if I just happen to be driving down an alley on garbage night, and I see a beautiful, old, hand-carved cabinet out by the trash, I just might happen to save it from the garbageman. Call it ecology or recycling if you want. I call it "junkshopping."

Of course, the polite thing to do is to knock on the owner's door and ask if you can have that "horrible old thing" as long as "they're throwing it out anyway." Never act too excited or they'll do one of three things: Call the police because they think you're a nut. Drag the cabinet back into the house. Or, charge you a healthy price.

Lucky me, the old cabinet that I dragged home turned out to be a very rare telephone cabinet. And the woman was kind enough to give me the tiny chair that goes with it, too. However, when my husband saw that beautiful piece of trash, he suggested we turn it into kindling for our fireplace. I knew better, because anything that looked that old and decrepit had to be valuable. So I scratched away some of the dark varnish with a fingernail file. Voila! Beneath all that gunk was gorgeous black walnut. It was time for me to do a strip!

Always work outside or in a well-ventilated area when stripping paint or varnish from wood. As a special precaution, I wear rubber gloves and sunglasses. I decided to do my stripping on the patio. A week later, a foot of grass died around the edge of our cement patio. Hubby didn't like that at all. And, furthermore, don't use stripper on an asphalt driveway. It bubbles to mush. It's best to strip on a cement garage floor with a water drain nearby.

Anyway, I replanted the grass, and stripped the cabinet and chair with one of the new water-soluble chemicals from the hardware store. There's nothing to this process. Briefly, you brush the chemical stripper on the surface you are lifting. Apply it thickly. Now wait 25 minutes or so, until the old varnish and paint appear to be loosening from the wood. Hose with clear water until all the old surface is removed. Sometimes a few bits of old paint cling to the wood. These must be retouched with stripper, or sanded off.

I bought a petite chair to match the telephone cabinet, also a Civil War-8 day clock. Total cost $25.00.

When the wood is completely dry (maybe two days later) sand gently with fine sandpaper. My secret formula for refinishing wood was found through necessity. I needed something inexpensive, expedient and durable to handle the second-hand furniture projects I brought home as a bride. It occurred to me that paste shoe polish was both a stain (color) and wax (sealer) in one inexpensive container. When applied with clean steel wool, paste shoe polish turned out to be the best refinisher I'd ever found. Incidentally, it takes about 48 hours to dry. Best of all, if your furniture gets scratches or burns, you can cover these with a smidget of shoe polish.

Antique investors and professional collectors remove, or have removed, old paint and heavy varnish to enrich the item and increase its intrinsic value. Naturally, cash is at the back of their mind. You should do the same, remembering that any antique wood should permit the lovely wood grain to show.

Refinished, my telephone cabinet and chair were a treasure. But, practical as always, I wanted them to have a function. Because this cabinet had vertical slots for telephone books and a French phone, and a drawer for pencils and stuff, I turned it into a file cabinet for my various (ahem) businesses. I've been told that the original French phone was brass and is very hard to find. Imagine how delighted I was when hubby gave me a music box copy of just such a phone. It was hard to believe he'd wanted to turn my treasure into fire wood!

Terrariums are terribly over priced. That's because most people don't know how to make them. It's really quite simple, you'll learn as you read my book.

Chapter 8
It's "Junkshopping" Time

About November, many of you begin to spot the signs of Christmas and may even groan to yourself, "O, no, not Christmas already!"

But for me, this is the middle of the Christmas season, for Labor Day marks the beginning of my fall "junk" shopping. To find inexpensive odds and ends that can be made into useful or decorative Christmas gifts, I rise at dawn once a week from early September to mid-December and slip out of the house while the milkman is still making his rounds.

Armed with a $5 bill and hubby's cheerful "good lucks," I nose the car toward an antique shop, near or far, depending on my whim. Riding shotgun to see that Mom doesn't come home with another 80-year-old, 300-pound water fountain (like I did last March) are Terra, Troy, Tamma an Baby Michael. Also, Wolf, our family Collie.

But six years ago, when I first started junkshopping, there were days when the items in antique shops looked like nothing but junk. From lack of use, my imagination had grown stale.

Fortunately, imagination is like sterling silver—the more it's used, the brighter it gets.

Even a modern brass chandelier can acquire traditional Christmas elegance with the addition of preserved evergreens, candy canes and candles. The preserving formula follows soon.

61

Last year, by mid-November, there were already a dozen red and green packages stacked on the highest shelf in our hall closet. The narrow, rectangular box contained a spice rack for someone special who enjoys chefing as a hobby.

I remember finding that spice rack despite the gloom in a wonderful junk barn in the western suburbs of Chicago. Even now, I can almost smell the odors that clung to everything there. A heady mixture of sawdust, dry leaves, and succulent apples, it made me think of Indians, pioneers and the exciting possibility of discovering a beloved treasure that had been carted westward by a covered wagon.

For ten minutes, I stared at that spice rack before I made up my mind to buy it. During that time, I noticed that the surface was scarred, yet the construction sturdy. Mentally, I visualized how a solution of two parts boiled linseed oil mixed with one part turpentine would cover the scratches. At the same time, it would bring out the wood's grain and leave a protective finish.

It was the narrow drawer along the bottom of the rack that definitely decided me, though. Couldn't that drawer serve as a recipe file? Certainly, I thought, and the recipes could utilize the spices above in exotic dishes that would appeal to . . . my dad, who else!

In an old hotel in Texas, I bartered for a solid maple Key rack. Voila! Each pigeon hole is perfect to hold small herb and spice jars.

I can't recall which came first, the idea for a tavern sign for my brother's malt shop or the gold-leaf picture frame I discovered while sleuthing in Old Town. Whichever it was, the two seemed to be made for each other. That's how simple it is for some gift ideas to be born—if you keep in mind the tastes and needs of the people you're shopping for.

There were two problems, however. The picture needed color, and the backing on the frame was in such terrible shape that it had to be covered. I solved both by gluing a square of bright red cloth over the backing. Using a stencil of early English style lettering, I cut from black felt the letters to spell, Ye Olde Malt Shop—Proprietor, Mack Milner.

Then one wintry evening, while the carols crooned softly from the TV set and the whole family gathered round to watch, I glued the felt letters to the cloth within the frame.

Like my husband, I love the sea. Sailing ships, to us, are great seagulls, free to swoop to the tropic isles we dream of visiting. Several Decembers ago, just before Michael was born, I decided to make hubby a windjammer. But, landlocked in six inches of midwestern snow, he'd have to settle for a model of one.

At first sight, you'd never guess that the hull of this model ship originated from a dried palm frond. The sails came from my worn-out oil cloth picnic table cloth.

For a hull, I used a long, long, gracefully curving palm frond I'd found on a bargain table in Elmhurst. I cradled this in a squat, four-legged stand that had previously held fancy jelly jars. Drilling a hole thru the bottom of the frond, I raised a mast—a length of whiplike floral bamboo. I painted the ship gold and shaded it black where the waves would cast their shadows, had it been launched on a miniature ocean. I was just cutting the sails from an old canvas picnic cloth . . . Then it was time to go to the hospital to have our baby. Before leaving the house, I tossed my hobby paints, scissors, turpentine, rags, brushes, linseed oil, picture wire, needle, thread, and the picnic cloth into my suitcase, on top of my new robe and slippers.

The next day, I rocked our sweet, rosy-cheeked son in hands that were splotchy with paint. Michael didn't seem to mind.

By the time we left the hospital, the sails were completed. I smuggled them home in my suitcase. Painted a mottled swirl of sunset, richly antiqued with gold, the sails seemed to be filled with a salty breeze because I'd stitched picture wire around the outer edges.

This, the most beautiful creation I've ever made, was my Christmas gift to dad—a windjammer that would sail the seas of his imagination forever.

My mother enjoys junkshopping as much as I do. Consequently, it was difficult to think up a Christmas present for her. Then one evening while dad and I were wandering through the art shops in Old Town, I discovered collages.

Knowing only that I wanted to find several frames that could be attractively arranged into a picture wall, I nosed northward to new hunting grounds in Evanston. I found four pine frames for $1. In my garage workshop, I antiqued these, successfully hiding their imperfections. From a discarded felt skirt, I made new backings to cover the yellowed cardboard in the frames.

I keep a cabinet for my vases and my miscellaneous items that might come in handy for making centerpieces or gifts. In this I found several leathery, maroon-colored maple leaves. I glued them to the felt in in one frame, with orange, pinkred, and gold paper copies of elm, oak and willow leaves. The effect was bright and free, as though the leaves were floating in midair. It's called, "Indian Summer."

My mom, Mrs. Alice Peters, and I often enjoy doing "junkshopping" projects together. Below, we're transforming an old coal bucket into a charcoal briquet holder for her patio.

65

The next collage, "Spring," depicts a line of stylized crocus blossoms. I cut these from shiny, enamel paint swatches, and drew the stems and leaves with a black dry-marker. To carry out the horizontal lines, I glued a parade of real snail shells, biggest to smallest, beneath the crocus.

The third collage was born out of my curiosity about macaroni. Somewhere, I'd read that macaroni takes on beautiful characteristics when gilded with spray paint. I thought it worth a try. I mixed four types of uncooked macaroni in a paper bag, spread a thick layer of glue over the backing in a frame, and poured the macaroni on. When I sprayed—Ala Kazaam!—gleaming baubles in "Neptune's Treasure Chest."

Another striking collage can be made by tracing the family's hands on a large sheet of cardboard. We did ours with dad's hand first, then mine overlapping his, Terra's overlapping mine, then Troy's, Tamma's and, last, Michael's. I painted these handprints orange and gold to complement our living room color scheme. To give an antique effect, I charred the picture's edges with a candle flame. Framing it in a wormy, weathered pie-shell frame, we now have an accessory that is truly a conversation piece.

A great way to use your not-so-good family snapshots is to make a photograph collage. They make excellent gifts for grandparents, too. Cut an assortment of photos into irregular shapes, and paste them to a background of your choice. Add the smaller ones last, some overlapping others. Seal with spray shellac.

There are certain inexpensive items that all antique and junk shops keep on hand. These are baskets and crocks. Baskets can be found, two for $1 or so, in every size, shape, and color. Occasionally, you'll run across a good-sized basket that's been bleached silver white by the weather. If you need a gift for someone with modern or oriental decor, buy one of these and fill it with smooth, white pebbles (available at most floral shops if you can't find them at the beach.)

Push the trunk of an interesting tree branch down into the pebbles until it's secure. With this "oriental tree," give the suggestion that it be displayed before a scroll painting or a decorative screen. The recipient is sure to be amazed at your resourcefulness.

Before you can say, "St. Nicholas," Christmas will be upon us, bringing with its December month a hassle of family birthdays—my mom's, Troy's, Tamma's, Michael's and mine. As you can see, between Thanksgiving and mid-January, we need a continual flow of decorations, gifts, and energy. That's why, early fall must be, for me, the real beginning of Christmas. Otherwise, I might not be done making presents in time to share that gift that's created in the heart — love.

If you can't find a real hi-button shoe, I'll show you how to turn any old shoe and a plastic detergent bottle into a lovely hi-button shoe vase.

Men junkshop, too! In fact, antique and junkshop owners, like the gentlemen below, will often become your very good friends.

For hours, the highway had threaded through thorns, rocks, and windswept plains. Only the craggy peaks of Big Bend National Park, snaking along the Rio Grande, protruded above the horizon. Huge rainless clouds raced our car toward the mirage that, rapidly, materialized into little Marfa, Texas.

When, at last, we arrived at the rustic Paisano (Roadrunner) Hotel, I sat for a moment, sensing the timelessness of this quaint, old, cow town. Any second, I expected thousands of longhorns to thunder through the wide, dusty streets, past the ostentatious, "1886," courthouse, to the Southern Pacific's shipping pens.

Forever a junkshopper, once in the lobby, I treasured the ancient terra cotta tile floors and walls. Later, I learned that Ft. Davis' First Cavalry had mule-trained these tiles from Chihuahua, Mexico, in 1920, despite attacks from Pancho Villa's Mexican bandits. Luckily, several European immigrants were weary of their rough railway jobs. They had grabbed at the chance to return to their "old country" traditions.

Painstakingly, they had cut and grouted the tiles. Artistically, they had carved huge, pine logs into ceiling timbers. As a last elegant touch, they had installed a relic from the Mayan ruins—an alabaster mantle and fireplace. The total effect was cool, serene, gracious, and, again, timeless.

It had seemed unlikely that a business trip to remote Marfa, Texas would prove to be exciting. But, with all these beautiful antiques, and some mighty interesting "junk," to boot, things were looking up!

For example: On the stucco ceiling above my bed, an old, metal and wood fan circulated hypnotically. There was no doubt that it produced far less cool air than the air conditioning. But, it tripped my mind, romantically, to film sets in Tahiti, Puerto Rico, Hong Kong . . . .

I had seen new copies of these old British fans selling for approximately $250.00 in decorator shops. Now, I wanted one. It would add a touch of intrigue to the outdoor dining lanai at our Beverly Hills home.

Since barter, or exchange, is almost always "second nature" to "junkies," I presented a fair swap to the Hotel manager, a few interior decorator hints for the fan. When we had loaded an old fan in the trunk of the car, I headed to the hotel's rustic bar, The Cattleman's Club, for a triumphant drink.

There, I noticed the brands that had been burned into the pine walls of the Cattleman's Club, my geiger counter zoomed again. Brands mean branding irons. And, believe it or not, a rusty, old branding iron is a "junkie's" delight!

There are many creative possibilities from these old irons. My favorite is to turn them into novel candelabras. Do this simply by standing the iron on its "branding" end, and inserting a candle of the appropriate circumference, in the hollow "handle" end. Of course, you'll want to clean it up first.

My secret recipe for rust removal: Soak metal or iron in equal parts apple cider vinegar and water for three days. Scrub vigorously with a soap pad. Dry thoroughly. Seal either by rubbing with raw steak fat, or spraying with rust preventative paint.

My friends in the East will probably have some difficulty finding branding irons. However, I've purchased several in the Chicago area; prices ranging from $7. and up. They're readily available in California and Texas, $3. and up, depending on the notoriety of the registered brand.

A closer examination of the brands revealed many famous settlers. For instance, there was the Mitchell family's mashed ( ) brand, registered in 1880. Today, Hayes Mitchell heads the Rio Grande Cattle Company from offices at the Paisano Hotel. There was the Bishop Brothers "1888" Heart ( ) Brand; Worth Evans "1890" Dry Moon ( ); L.C. Brite's "1890" Forty-six ( ), and Theron Johnson's "1885" Dipper ( ) Brand. Of course, there were others. But, these names have been active in the West for generations.

"DONATED NOV. 8, 1928, BY PRESIDENT FULLER, MARFA CHAMBER OF COMMERCE." The brass plate on the quaint, French safe commemorated the day that Marfa decided to expand its population by enticing tourists and cowmen with a real, honest to goodness, hotel. According to the Big Bend Sentinel, "The citizens were so anxious to have a steel-reinforced, two-story building, with circulating water, and the very best dance floor in this section of Texas, that the Chamber of Commerce solicited donations from prominent citizens."

There was no way to pry that priceless safe from the hotel manager. He said that it was just as functional today, as it had been in 1928—a safe place to store valuables. Neither listened to my pleas that "antique safes make very novel, handy, cocktail bars." For now, maybe they're right. But, tomorrow the safe will probably be more valuable as a miniature bar!

Near the safe, on an old stucco wall, hung a rack for mail and hotel keys. In seconds, I pictured that valuable oak wood stripped and refinished. The rack would, or could, become a gorgeous "gigantic" spice shelf.

I could see that this mail rack was used constantly for just what it was made for. So, I tactfully didn't make an offer. However, I vowed to find one, "someday." And . . . I'm still looking!

When our host asked me to complete my end of the "fan" bargain by advising him how to freshen the stuffed deer and buffalo heads in the hotel's lobby, I was delighted. In fact, it reminded me of one of the first times I went "junkshopping" back in Chicago . . .

As usual, I only had $5. with me, and I needed, or wanted, fifty things. In an especially dusty, moldy, mysterious "junkshop" I saw an old bear skin hanging in a corner.

Trying to act "cool," I looked it over with apparent disdain and grumbled, "How much for this old thing?"

Knowing the price of bearskin rugs, I thought the proprietor was rather dumb when she told me that I could have it for five bucks. Soon, I discovered that she knew just what she was doing.

You can't imagine how thrilled I was to bring that lovely old fur to my new suburban home, and throw it on the floor next to the masterbed. It seemed, "Just like a dream, a movie set, or a decorator's magazine." But, it was true! Then, I noticed the terribly foul odor all around me. Could it come from my treasure? Further investigation revealed that it did, and, like . . . wow!

When I took my rather unluxurious fur to a famous furrier in Hinsdale, he took one look and stated that he wouldn't touch it. Later, he explained that it was terribly old; would undoubtedly fall apart in cleaning. He asked me if I realized that that wasn't a rug at all. It was a sleigh blanket! Lucky me, I had a genuine, antique sleigh blanket . . . with a deodorant problem.

When I got home, I filled the bathtub with icy cold water. I poured in a cup of cold-water soap and threw the rug in. Slush! Slush! Slush! It truly stank now. But, I stuck it out. The water was muddy, black, filthy, when I hauled the rug out. Sponging with bathtowels, I managed to remove at least half the water. Then, I drug it downstairs and out to the patio. With great effort, I managed to hang it on our privacy fence to dry.

Three days later, it had dried thoroughly. To my delight, my treasure smelled like a rose. Now all it needed was a little fluffing up with the vacuum. So, I hauled the vacuum outside, plugged it in, and started. In minutes, there were only three hairs left on a stiff leather board. I was crushed. In fact, I almost gave up "junkshopping!!!"

But, instead, I learned from an antique cookbook that the way to clean old furs (and hairpieces, as a matter of fact) is to sprinkle equal parts borax and white cornmeal onto the skin. Let it sit half an hour or so, then remove with a vacuum. This simple technique cleans, freshens and restores the furs to most of their former brilliance.

"Never, ever use water," I cautioned our hotel host. And he promised not to.

As you can see, it's easy to transform three small kegs into a rustic mailbox.

Patched levi pants, jackets, coats and hats are current "with-it" fashions. Just another example of a reverse snobbery trend in America.

Chapter 10
"Junkshopping" from A to Z

On the way back to California, I noticed another unique Texan "junk-shop" creation. This unexpected mailbox is made by hammering two nail kegs together, one on top of the other, to form a stand. Next, attach a third nailkeg sitting across the stand on its side.

Hinge the top so the door can swing open to accept the mail. You now have the most rustic mailbox around!

Just the reverse of this idea, a few years ago, I turned my aluminum mailbox into an umbrella stand. It all started because our neighborhood finally qualified for door to door mail. I took down that big, trusty mailbox, and instead of throwing it away, turned it into a planter.

Later, I thought of the umbrella-cane stand for my foyer. To make it was simple enough—simply spray paint, allow to dry, and spray with hairspray to preserve. Now dip twine in liquid starch and glue. Press onto the box in patterns of your taste. I used flower centers, petals, leaves and many twining vines. When dry, hand-paint with a stripe of oils along all the patterns. Or, paint with many shades of oils.

Also in Texas, I first noticed what actually originated in California—groovy new coats, hats, purses, dresses and suits made from many, many pairs of old levis. The artistry, naturally, comes from the careful design-ing and tailoring of these items to gain maximum nostalgia.

According to my clothes designer, my friend, Reuben Bayetto, "There is no way to accomplish this design with minimum effort. It takes time and labor."

If you wish to try it yourself—you must, first, buy ten or twelve pairs of old jeans at swapmeets. The cheaper the better. Now, cut very worn spots away, leaving sturdy material. Reuben says he likes to leave some holes in the garments to patch later on. It adds additional character. When your large levi sections are sewed together, make a silk or cotton lining. Again, Reuben uses bright prints to recapture an early Americana look. Add brass buttons, belts, trim, stitching at the collar, and you've got it— the reverse snobbery, elegant "junkshopper" look.

Potpourri of Sari's Creations

When I started "junkshopping" about 8 years ago, everyone thought I was crazy. Now everyone "junkshops" and they understand my enthusiasm.

A tiny coal stove from a caboose can either be a large size hibachi, a planter or the base of an end table.

Once again my hi-button shoe steals the show. This time it was displayed on a national T.V. show.

Performances for women's clubs and organizations (and sometimes for men's too) has kept me busy, once or twice a week for nearly 8 years. It just shows the current interest in "junkshopping" all over the world.

A lovely sterling silver chastity purse has become one of my favorite accessories. It makes a charming evening bag.

A $2.50 white elephant from a garage sale turned out to be one of the first light fixtures made in America. Too bad I didn't save the original old bulb and wiring. It would be worth a fortune!

Believe it or not, this (ahem) quaint item is commonly called a "flying duck." I use it for a planter.

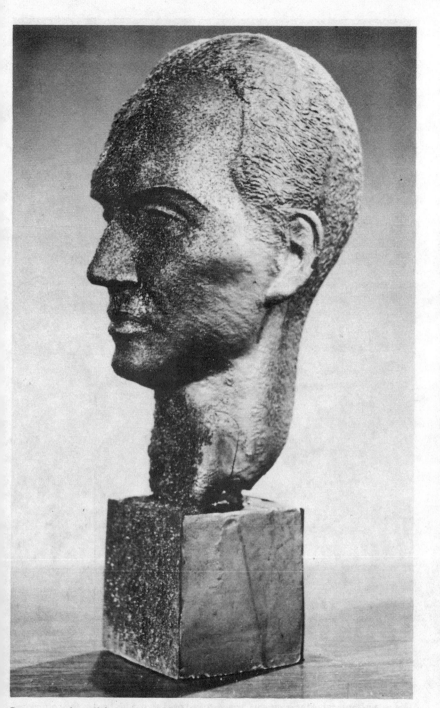

George was a beautiful statue . . . with many chips and cracks. I fixed him up better than new with paint and a sprinkling of table salt. Paint again.

This valuable lunch bucket is called a "grauer." Dad used to put his beer in the bottom half, his sandwich on top. I turned it into a purse; cosmetics on the bottom, check book and wallet on top.

Mom and I bought several old lanterns at an auction. Rejuvenated and electrified, they make darling lamps.

A 25¢ wooden shoe form, hand painted with oils, hangs on brass hooks on my front door. Bang the toe and it's a clever door knocker.

A brass post office box door, cleaned with ammonia, makes a conversation piece when used as a picture frame.

Why not have your own Keyclub? Transform antique barrel keys into tie clips, necklaces, buttons, earrings and key chains. It's easy!

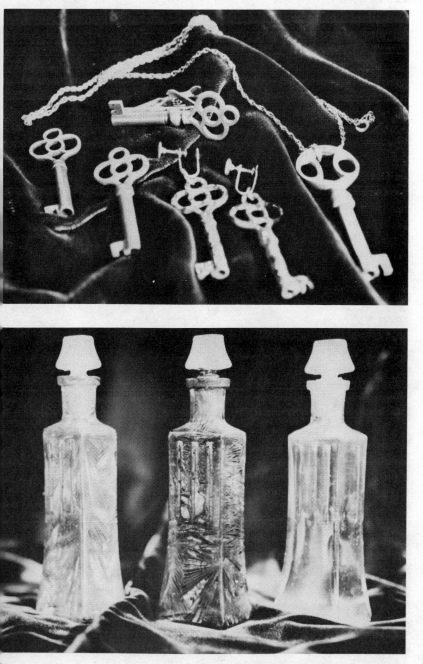

These antique perfume bottles were stained with liquid plastic. Later, I noticed that they were "Made in Japan" in 1964. But I love them anyway.

Postcards, bits of seaweed and matchbooks make a wonderful "vacation collage" especially when displayed in a genuine gardener's flat box.

have many restored statues around my home, but only two preserved trees. I'm sure you'll
gree that natural touches enrich any environment.

Before and after, an old electrical light fixture becomes a $50.00 brass candle sconce.

With so many children in the family, I needed a giant sized cookie jar. A well sterilized chamber pot was a more than adequate solution.

If you can find a hi-button shoe, restore it with shoe polish, preserve it with hair spray, push a baby bottle or a pilsner beer glass down inside and you have a lovely waterproof vase.

Nature lover or not, most of us are ecology minded today. I combed California beaches for bits of glass, seaweed, rocks, driftwood and shells to make my ecology collage.

gain from the beaches, I gathered **rocks** and shells and arranged them in thriftshop baskets.
rom a fascinating stump, I conjured **an end** table. My own dried flowers adorn everyroom in the
ouse.

Once you become ecology-minded, you won't want to see aluminum cans wasted. It's quite safe to cut them and turn them into candleholders and ashtrays.

Chapter 11
Applying Ecology to Junkshopping

Like most people, somewhere in the back of my mind I thought that all the resources on Mother Earth would never wear out. Then I began to hear distant warnings from T.V., radio, the press. Soon, there were out and out danger signals all around: Our earth was becoming polluted. And I, like everyone else, shook my head in disbelief. But we all know now that it's true—If we aren't prudent with nature's elements, and the by-products that man has made from these treasures, they'll soon be gone.

About three years ago, I was gazing out my front window at the angry, grey Pacific, and I vowed to recycle everything I possibly could. Maybe, if I could find a clever use for butter tubs, beer cans and cigarette wrappers, the beach would be clean again. I knew I would enjoy this because, like my hobby, "junkshopping," I would be helping preserve, or recycle Nature's elements. And I would be setting an example for my children and my neighbors.

Not that I hadn't always recycled things. Even as a student at the University of Colorado, I often wandered through dismal thrift shops in Denver, seeking rejuvenable items for my room at the Kappa Alpha Theta House. Usually discards like rusted record racks, old, cheap brass bookshelves, practical accessories, but things that aren't old enough to be desirable, were recyclable with a little effort. These "goodies" ended up in my little cubby hole room.

Necessity being the mother of invention, I soon learned that equal parts vinegar and water removed rust from metal, and household ammonia cleaned brass. If this didn't work, a one-dollar can of rust preventative paint covered any remaining imperfections. My sorority sisters complimented me on my furnishings, never realizing "from whence they came."

Old wicker, which is so very popular today, was dirt-cheap then. I remember dragging home an old wicker dressing table and stool. No amount of spray paint would cover those nooks and crannies. Through trial and error, I learned that wicker can best be repainted with a mixture of half-turpentine and half-paint. Incidentally, white-washed wicker, my set, was smashing against a lavender wallpaper background.

CLEVER ALUMINUM CAN CANDLEHOLDER

Recycle any aluminum can into a clever candleholder:

a. Just beneath the rim of a can, where the aluminum seems more pliable, carefully make a hole with scissors or an ice pick. Enlarge this hole until it will allow for the cutting action of medium-size scissors. As evenly as possible, cut the lid off.

b. Picture your can divided in half vertically, and make a vertical cut from the top to about 1-1/2 inches from the bottom. Make another, similar cut an inch away. Continue cutting vertically, 1-inch apart, until one half of the can is shredded, and the other half is solid. Usually, this produces four 1-inch strips of aluminum.

c. With the tip of the scissors, curl the first strip under, creating a spiral, like a snail shell. Do the same to the other three strips. Now, if you set a two to three inch high candle inside the can, you have a candleholder with an aluminum reflector behind it. In front, you have four decorative curls. With scissors, trim the edges of the reflector until they are safely and attractively rounded.

d. Cover the exterior of your can with colorful, gum-backed paper. Leave the curls and the interior natural. This will make it fire-safe, but attractive.

ATTRACTIVE ALUMINUM CAN ASHTRAY

To make an aluminum can into an ashtray, cut 1-inch strips all the way around the can and curl the strips under as in **CLEVER CANDLEHOLDER.** Cover the exterior of the base with gum-backed paper. Leave curls and aluminum interior natural to accommodate ashes and cigarettes.

EASY-DO ALUMINUM CAN RATTLE

To make an aluminum can into a baby's rattle, drop 1 tablespoon beans inside. Seal the top with heavy decorator tape. Cover the entire can with decorator tape stripes for a more attractive appearance. Of course, this rattle is washable with a damp cloth. Also, for older children, it can be used as a primitive musical instrument.

COASTER CRAFT

Shallow plastic catsup and mustard containers, enclosed in your kit,* can be "recycled" into coasters, mobiles, mini-pictures and Christmas ornaments.

a. Assemble any assorted family photos, decals, magazine pictures, drawings, business cards, awards, soup decals, labels, designs, collages, postcards, etc. that you have around the house. Set a round plastic con-

*"Sari's Junk Box" is available in toy and hobby departments.

tainer on the picture or card of your choice. Lightly outline it with pencil. Cut out.

b. Using the adhesive enclosed in your kit,* secure the picture to the inside bottom of one of the round plastic containers. Apply adhesive to the outer rim of that same container, then press a second container inside the first container. Hold until sealed.

c. Your photo, picture, or whatever, is now sealed between two layers of plastic. Use this as a clever coaster. In fact, make a set!

d. Follow the above steps to create a mobile. But, when your set of four coasters is finished, punch a small hole at the top of each. Tie a 12-inch length of heavy button thread to the hole in each coaster. Attach these at different levels to a coathanger, wooden dowels or two sticks. Tie the sticks together and hang from a high spot. You now have a mobile!

e. Double-edged tape, or gum-backed picture hangers that are sticky on both sides, are fun combined with your finished coaster-pictures. Simply attach to the back of the coaster, then press against the wall, or to a bulletin board. You now have a set of mini-pictures. Kids and teens will love this idea for their school lockers, cars, etc.

f. Recycle used Christmas cards by cutting them to fit between two plastic containers, as if making coasters. Add glitter, paints, ribbons, sequins, etc. Punch a hole at the top; tie with yarn or ribbon; and hang on your Christmas tree. Use your imagination; customize your ornaments! Why not seal a bit of holly or pine between two coasters?

Shallow plastic condiment holders make adorable "picture" coasters. Simply glue family snap shot in one, and another coaster on top.

95

My favorite "Sari Original" at the time was a steamer trunk that I had transformed into a dresser. When I found this treasure in an alley, the owner, a charming actress, said it was mine, totally free, if I would "preserve all the delightful memories inside."

Spray painted ivory, hand painted with blue and lavender flowers, and bright green leaves, my dresser was charming, useful and convenient. Not to mention, today, I still have this dresser and, believe me, it's doubled its "memory bank."

But what of all those small, apparently garbage items we have in our homes? The things that litter the beach, the highways, the parks? Well, I've turned a good deal of my attention, and my imagination to reactivating, and renovating these items, and I think you should, too. Why don't you give it a try? Watch in the next chapter . . .

Artificial flowers, tucked into birdcages of all sizes, add color and interest to dreary corners

It's easy to remove paint from any metal surface with furniture stripper. Never use this on aluminum or silver.

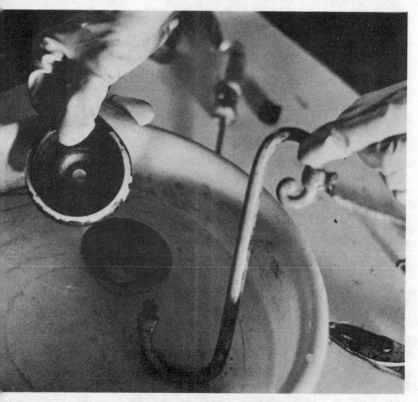

Remember to use a plastic container when you work with vinegar or furniture stripper.

Using my formula, dry your own flowers, and arrange them on driftwood or rocks. Add tiny figurines if you wish.

Chapter 12
Back to Nature

I've always had a penchant for bringing nature into my home. Since living in California, this has almost become an obsession. Aside from terrariums, through trial and error, I've learned reliable recipes for preserving plants and trees.

To dry your own flowers or field flowers: Mix ten cups white corn meal with two cups of borax. Sift about an inch of this dry mixture into a deep box. Gently lay your flowers on this, and cover with rest of mixture. You may make double batches of this formula, and use it over and over again. It never wears out. In four days, remove your flowers, and spray with plastic preservative, or hairspray, to help prevent breakage. It's possible to dip flowers that have lost a good deal of their color in ink. This restores natural color that spray paint can't achieve.

At a rummage sale, I had purchased an assortment of large baskets for approximately $1. each. Leaving them natural, I strung macramed twine from the ceiling to the baskets. When they were all hanging at different levels, brightening any dreary corners of my apartment, I arranged my dried flowers in huge bouquets. Now and then, I change the basket arrangements to suit the season.

I wanted a tree—a tree that would appear to be growing right in my livingroom. Artificial trees are expensive and, they look artificial. So, I canvassed my antique cookbooks for a formula. I found the answer in a recipe for preserving apple blossoms, cattails, pussywillows, and eucalyptus leaves in equal parts glycerin and water.

If this would work on other sap-fed branches, why not a whole tree? With a friend's permission, I cut down a young Russian Olive from an over-crowded grove. I set the stump in a two-quart can of antifreeze. Because, antifreeze is equal parts glycerin and water, and it's cheaper. Three days later, the sap in the tree had completely absorbed the antifreeze.

My lovely, oriental-looking Olive tree, with its dainty green leaves, lasted for three years. Never did it become brittle, a fire hazard, or attract termites. And, just as I had hoped, it appeared to be growing in a pot in my livingroom, surrounded by ocean-washed pebbles.

You'll love this formula for your Christmas tree. Follow the same directions, and you'll have your tree for eight months! I always place my little fir out on the patio in a planter, and everyone thinks it's growing. Of course, a live Christmas tree is even better.

Another time, I preserved grapevines and wrapped them around a privacy fence. These weathered high winds, earthquakes, and children. Always, my neighbors thought they were "alive," and the vines were just as beautiful three years later.

Troy, my oldest son, sewed preserved grapevines and leaves to a heavy cardboard. Naturally, he used a large needle and button thread. When he'd mounted the cardboard in a frame, he sprayed the whole thing gold. It's a gorgeous collage.

From the beach, the forest, the desert, I've brought hundreds of treasures into my home. For example: A dried-up Joshua tree, wired and sitting on a little stand, is a lovely floor lamp. We picked out a simple shade and covered it with macramed twine.

Stone end tables are a joke until you see them. Beautiful slabs of rock, when treated with a littled colored wax, make unique, ecology-minded end tables. I topped mine with weathered, preserved slabs of redwood. Once I even dragged home a whole tree stump. Preserved with glycerin and water, shellacked twenty times, this treasure is either a footstool, a stool or an end table, depending on the need.

I used to go to the beach, daily, gathering bits of driftwood, shells, seaweed and moss. When dried, I preserved these with hairspray. My favorite ecology collage began with a large slab of driftwood. I glued an assortment of my favorite beach shells, rocks, smooth glass, moss and seaweed in a natural pattern on the driftwood. When it had dried thoroughly, I sprayed with many coats of hairspray.

Next, I sculpted, yes, sculpted a large wad of bubble gum into the shape of a seagull. Days later, when it had hardened, I spray-painted it white, and hand-painted eyes and details. Attached to my "Sea" collage, it looks very artistic!

Today, we recycle attractive bottles simply by scrubbing them, and filling them with lovely, assorted rocks and shells. These make beautiful decanters for an executive's office. And, according to my dad, they're best displayed when filled with water.

I call them "rock babies" but they're really hand painted rocks. Do them yourself for a fresh, zesty look, for arrangements and collections.

Do you have a skimpy budget? You can still make your surroundings attractive. Example: the basket in the picture was 25¢. Flowers free for the making.

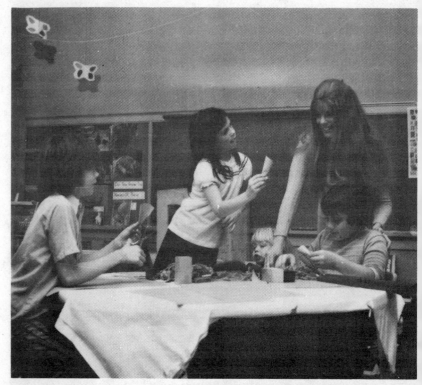

I was thrilled to become a teacher at my children's school. My subject? Naturally, it's "junk-shopping." What else? Children today are very much aware of ecology and recycling. Bless them! They know where it's at.

Chapter 13
The Egg and I

Consider the lowly egg carton. Believe it or not, cardboard egg cartons, and the cardboard separators that apples and oranges are packed in, make fantastic stereo speakers. The technique? Simply staple that part of the carton that holds the eggs to the wall, so the egg cups stick out.

Cover this wall, or walls opposite each other, with cartons. Leave no wall-space between the cartons, but make designs if you wish. Now spray-paint the cartons on the wall, solidly. Voila! They make a really striking sculptured effect. Not only that, according to stereo experts I've talked with, the cartons provide the best speaker sound you can buy.

Rummaging further through my kitchen garbage can, I find egg shells —a poor, humble friend we all have in our homes. Immediately, I can think of three or four marvelous ideas for egg shells.

For example: My students wanted an idea for a Halloween decoration, so I created a pumpkin or witch from a hollow egg. With an ice pick, poke a tiny hole at either end of your eggs. Blow gently into the top hole, so that the inside of the egg comes out the bottom hole into a bowl. When I had emptied all of my eggs in this way, I had a bowl full of eggs which I could use for scrambled eggs or an omelet. I had another bowl full of empty, perfectly whole egg shells. Now I rinsed these in cool water, and gently shook them dry.

The kids painted the eggs with orange Tempera paints. With Garter Glue, they stuck pumpkin seeds on the eggs for eyes, a kernel of corn for a nose, a tiny row of black peppercorns for a grim-looking mouth. To display their mini-sculptures securely, each child cut a section from the egg carton, and painted it black. They set the egg in this, and it resembled a collar. Some took the pointed portion of the egg carton, painted it black, too, and set it on top of the egg to create a witch's hat. Others made hats out of different pieces of cardboard and felt. When finished, pumpkins were wearing berets, or ten-gallon western hats. If you can imagine how adorable these little pumpkins and witches were . . . Well, the school asked if they could display them in the glass cases in the library. We were very proud, my little junkshoppers, and me . . .

Again, at Halloween, the class also enjoyed making our Halloween skeleton. For this, we baked little pieces of biscuit dough until very dark brown. When cool, we sprayed them with hairspray to preserve the dough. I attached a piece of twine to a small nail, and stuck it in the bottom of the biscuit, so I had a head and a long piece of twine hanging down from it.

Now, from the grocery store, I bought rigatoni noodles. Of course, they were uncooked, and about one half inch wide, oval shaped, and about three inches long each. The children strung the rigatoni on the twine making the trunk of a skeleton. They tied other pieces of twine to the trunk for arms and legs. Naturally, they strung a rigatoni for each of these. We used round, small noodles for hands and feet, and any joints on the rest of the body.

When the little skeleton was finished, we hung him on twigs, so that he was actually a puppet. You could jiggle him and his arms and legs would dance. For eyes, again we glued on pumpkin seeds, corn for the nose, and a row of pepper corns for teeth.

During the holidays, the children used the egg shell idea for ornaments. It was easy to glue scraps of felt, material, old sequins or rick-rack, even ribbon, to empty egg shells. They created lovely patterns that made gorgeous, one-of-a-kind ornaments for a Christmas tree.

Later, in a new project, we crushed egg shells and glued them solidly to non-returnable glass bottles. Boy, the Park Board thanked us for cleaning up all those old bottles from the park grounds. You ought to give it a try—improve your local park, and at the same time, acquire glass bottles for craft projects.

When the glue had dried, and the egg shells on the bottle were secure, the children spray-painted them with gold. While the paint was still wet, they sprinkled on gold glitter.

The children inserted a candle at the top of the bottle, wrapped a red ribbon around it, added a greeting card, and, once again, a piece of true junk had become a joy. This time, in the form of a beautiful holiday candle as a Christmas gift for mom and dad.

It's absolutely marvelous to "find" an idea that everyone can copy from discards in their home. A creation that is elegant, despite it's humble origins, one that permits each individual the full scope of his imagination, is extremely timely in our ecology minded society. I didn't realize that I had hit on such an item until weeks after this "original" was comfortably ensconced in my home.

It all began when I bid for a double-bucket, center-handled oddity at the Saugus-Newhall swapmeet. For $1.50, I figured that I had a unique galvanized planter—ivy on the one side; geraniums on the other.

But, I needed new cannisters . . . and, "bingo," these would make perfect FLOUR and SUGAR containers. Patchwork, utilizing scraps of material dipped in liquid starch, or pieces of gum-backed paper, would give me maximum color and nostalgia. This is a simple process, and one I prefer to spray painting, for smaller accessories.

After a thorough scrubbing, I lined the buckets with aluminum foil. Now, I needed lids. The lumber yard supplied two rounds of 1/2 inch plywood for 50 cents each.

Bread, pretzels, rolls, cookies are very "in" right now as wall hangings and "bread baskets." I'd been making Christmas ornaments from sugar cookies preserved with hair spray, for years. My imagination tripped again—why not say FLOUR with a legible combination of round and straight pretzels?

And, to hide that humble plywood lid, I smoothed ready-made biscuit dough over the plywood and around the wood-dowel handle. Now, I baked wood and dough according to directions, until the lid was an appetizing brown. When cool, I sprayed it with many coats of plastic preservative. You may also use hairspray, if it's more convenient.

As a finishing touch, I glued macrame strips of packing twine around the outer edge of the lid, and the bucket's base.

Oh, what a glory! Imagine this yummy combination—colorful, nostalgic patchwork; unique, charming pretzels, and dough; rich, earthy macrame. I loved it! You will, too.

But, what about the sugar? You guessed it—Why not use sugar cubes!

Glued down to spell sugar on the front, and to solidly cover the wooden lid, they're adorable. Definitely preserve these with hairspray.

Let your imagination take off . . . You don't have to begin your cannisters with buckets. Even better, recycle juice cans, and vegetable cans, using the same techniques for transforming them into cannisters.

For example: A RICE storage cannister is adorable with RICE written with toothpicks. Ah so! And, of course, uncooked rice glued and sprayed to the lid tells the whole story.

Can you imagine coffee—Coffee beans of course! How about kidney-beans, corn, sunflower seeds, candy? And, cannister sets are perfect gift items. There's no end to the uses—storage for nails, crayons, electrical parts, thumb tacks, etc. The rest is up to you.

Crocks, whether new or old, are adorable, as well as useful, when turned into cannisters. It's the little decorator's touches that make the difference.

Add dried rice to the wooden lid of a cannister that will store rice. Coffee beans for one that will store coffee and etc. Seal with hair spray.

TIDY-CAN STORAGE CONTAINERS

Any tin can can be "recylced" into an efficient, attractive cannister or storage container. However, for practical purposes, we've chosen the three most commonly-found can sizes and enclosed lids for them in this kit.

a. Gather a fruit juice can, or any can that is 2lb. 8oz. to 3 lb., a tomato or bean can that is 1lb. 12oz. and a dogfood or vegetable can that is 15 oz. Wash, rinse and dry.

b. Enclosed in your kit* are many colorful patches. Also, a plastic container of adhesive with an easy-to-use, roll-on-type applicator. In addition, we've provided scraps of trim. You'll merely need scissors and imagination to complete this project.

c. Rub a heavy coating of adhesive on the back of a patch. Press anywhere on one of your three cans. Hold for a second, then repeat the same procedure with another patch. Bear in mind that your goal is to completely cover every bit of tin can with patches. Similarly, cover the lids with patches.

d. When all three cans are covered, cut the trim to fit around the top and the bottom of each of your three cans. Glue on.

e. To make a clever knob design from twist-off bottle caps, assemble three bottle caps, and patches and glue adhesive from your kit.* Now decide what you wish to store in each cannister. If it's candy, half-way fill the bottle cap with glue. Drop in tiny candies, such as Red Hots, seeing that the cap is filled to overflowing and that all pieces are glued. While the candies are drying clear, cut a patch to fit around the exterior of the bottle cap. Glue on snugly. Again, using glue, attach the knob to the finished lid. Allow to dry at least 24 hours.

f. As a last touch, spell the word CANDY on the front of your cannister by glueing tiny candies to shape the letters, or by glueing on birthday cake letter decorations.

*"Sari's Junk Box" is available in toy and hobby departments.

g. If you're going to store popcorn in another cannister, follow the same procedure, but fill the bottle cap with popped popcorn, instead of candy. And, spell POPCORN with raw popcorn kernels on the front of the cannister. For a flour cannister, bake a tiny bit of biscuit dough in the bottle cap. When cool, wrap with a patch and spray with hairspray to preserve the biscuit. With scissors, cut the word FLOUR from a raw tortilla. Glue on the front of the cannister and spray with hairspray. Now you can really use your imagination—imagine a COFFEE cannister, DRIED BEANS cannister, RICE, even NAILS, SCREWS, NUTS and BOLTS, etc. Almost anything can be utilized in a clever cannister project. Have fun!

One of the most humble items in your home, tin cans, will readily become containers and/or cannisters. Why not make a set?

You can preserve even fresh flowers with a few drops of glycerin in the water.

Chapter 15
"A Boot to Boot"

Of all the "Sari Originals" in the world, after my four wonderful children—Terra (13), Troy (11), Tamma (9) and Michael (3)—I love my "hi-button shoe" creation. At best, it's difficult for experts to find these treasures. Call it beginner's luck, but one day, when I had finally needled dad into joining me on a junkshopping jaunt, he found one.

I couldn't believe it when he took this dusty, squashed hi-button shoe from beneath a pile of old table legs.

"This looks like it died years ago," he grinned. "Can you take a real "junkshopper" challenge? Let's see you turn it into something."

Even more unbelievable, he walked over to the shopkeeper and placed two dollars by the cash register. "This'll more than cover me taking this off your hands."

Shopkeep thoughtfully chewed a wad of tobacco. He winked at me, and nodded affirmatively at hubby. When we got to the car, I nearly exploded with delight. Boy **could** I turn that into something!

The task of rejuvenating the shoe turned out to be much simpler than I had anticipated. First, I reshaped the boot by squeezing wads of newspaper into the narrow pointed toes. The ankle and upper calf portion were naturally shaped when I inserted a baby bottle down inside.

The dry leather responded to many coats of black paste shoe polish. With heavy button thread, I sewed on all loose buttons. Now, so the shoe would forever hold its "band box" appearance, I sprayed with coat after coat of liquid plastic.

When hubby sat down to dinner that night, he was suddenly speechless. There, as a table centerpiece, sat a lovely, shiny, black hi-button shoe, brimming at the top with a bouquet of fresh, red roses.

Of course, I explained to him that the baby bottle inside holds the water and the flower stems. He was terribly impressed, and I was proud, proud, proud. . .

Later, I used that same boot, always with different flower arrangements, as my trademark on my daily T.V. show, "Sari the Junkshopper." Still later, after I'd moved to California, bringing my boot along, of course, I used it as a class project at Everywoman's Village.

My "junkshopping" students at the "Village" were all sophisticated women seeking new creative ideas. If I said, "Next week, class, we're going to create a hi-button shoe vase like this one," they'd go out that very afternoon seeking hi-button shoes. We were all disappointed when only one student could come up with the necessary shoe after a week of searching. And though hers was a lace-up type hi-button shoe, it responded beautifully to my instructions for the vase treatment.

I had to do something for these marvelous, enthusiastic gals, so I created a boot. In case you want to try it, here's the recipe:

Purchase a plastic bottle of liquid detergent, medium size. See that your bottle has a larger base, curving to a smaller top. When the contents have been emptied, rinse, and save.

Meanwhile, buy an old high heel shoe, with the passe' type pointed toe. These are 10 cents at most thrift shops. Gather newspaper, rip it into long 1-inch wide strips. Mix together enough flour and water to make a paste the thickness of medium whitesauce. Add approximately two teaspoons white glue to each cup of paste, and stir.

Wad balls of newspaper and squeeze into the toe of your shoe. Cut the bottom off the plastic detergent bottle. Leave the lid screwed on the top. Set the bottle upside down in the shoe, so that the detergent bottle resembles the ankle-calf portion of a hi-button shoe. Tape into place.

Dip strips of newspaper in paste and wrap around hi-heel and detergent bottle, smoothing carefully. When totally covered, your creation resembles a hi-button shoe. Add two more coats of paper mache'. Allow to dry for up to forty-eight hours.

At this point, use your imagination to visualize how you want your boot to look. Do you want to paint it, or patchwork quilt it with material scraps or sticky-backed paper scraps? You'll probably want to glue a double row of buttons down the front, like a real hi-button shoe. Or, maybe, dip shoe laces in glue and criss-cross them down the front, like a hi-button lace-up shoe. A bit of starched lace, glued around the boot top, is very feminine. So are bows.

Because I wanted a bright accessory, and I had many scraps of material at home, I patchworked my boot. I cut my materials into all sizes and shapes, dipped each piece into liquid starch, and smoothed it onto the boot. When totally covered, and thoroughly dried, I glued on laces, buttons, ribbons and lace. Since the detergent bottle is waterproof, again I arranged a bouquet of fresh flowers in my hi-button shoe vase.

Incidentally, these make adorable gifts when filled with wrapped, hard candies. And, excellent doorstops, when loaded with pebbles.

After my program, women swarm around me asking for "tips" and advice on "junkshopping." Well, I've included them in this book . . . and more.

SARI'S HI-BUTTON SHOE

A plastic bottle and any old boot or shoe can be "recycled" into a charming, waterproof vase that resembles an antique hi-button shoe:

a. Use a plastic bottle, such as a liquid detergent or a shampoo bottle. See that your bottle has a larger base, curving to a smaller top. Replace the cap and be sure that it is screwed on tightly.

b. Find an old boot or shoe that, when your plastic bottle is turned upside down in it, resembles the outline of a hi-button shoe. For example: A small plastic shampoo bottle and a baby's shoe would make a darling miniature hi-button shoe. A woman's pointed-toe hi-heel and a medium-size liquid detergent bottle would make a charming replica of a genuine hi-button shoe. A man's boot and a large plastic bottle would make a giant-size hi-button shoe.

c. Whatever size plastic bottle you have decided on, carefully cut the bottom off in an even line. Rinse thoroughly inside and out.

d. Anchor the plastic bottle, with the cap screwed on tightly, upside down in the boot or shoe with many, many strips of tape such as adhesive, masking or electrical tape. Cover all open spaces with tape, so that the detergent bottle and shoe are joined together solidly.

e. Mix Calcora Decor with water until it becomes the texture of thick frosting. Add more water, if needed, a tablespoon at a time. Do not allow the mixture to become watery. Using a butter knife, "frost" the shoe and detergent bottle with a solid, even coating of the Calcora Decor. When the shoe and bottle are completely coated, you'll see that there's no doubt you have created a hi-button shoe.

f. While the "frosting" is still moist, cut ribbon (from your kit*) to wrap around the top and the heel of your hi-button shoe. And you may wish to push a strip of ribbon down the back or along the toe. Criss-cross ribbon to resemble laces down the front. You may add buttons, or anything your imagination creates when working with Calcora Decor.

g. Allow to dry for two days in a medium temperature. When dry, patch any tiny cracks with a small amount of Calcora Decor. Now you may add water and fresh flowers. Or, an attractive arrangement of artificial flowers. Whatever, you're going to be thrilled with this unusual creation.

*"Sari's Junk Box" is available in toy and hobby departments.

Most of my adult classes have had difficulty finding hi-button shoes. We created a nearly as charming prototype from any old shoe and a plastic detergent bottle.

Chapter 16

Soap Sculpture for Ecology's Sake

My soapshow village made from soap-frosted cardboard figures, is still a family Christmas favorite, eight years later.

Would you believe that this solid brass roulette cage makes a knockout planter?

A centerpiece of brightly-colored soap fruits adds a cheerful note to mealtimes and a sweet fragrance to a winter-tight kitchen. You'll need a box of any white detergent, water, wood coloring, and a lively imagination to begin this hobby.

Pour an amount of detergent into a bowl and add tablespoons of water, stirring all the while, until you have a mixture the consistency of soft clay. Using food coloring, tint the soap-clay the color of the fruit you plan to make.

Begin to shape your fruit by rolling the soap into a tight ball. Handling it as little as possible, work the ball into the shape of the fruit you are making.

Make stems and leaves of green-colored soap-clay. Attach the stems with straight pins, press the leaves to the stems, and hold until partially hardened.

Make grapes of small balls of clay and string them on a thread with a needle. When they are dry, arrange them in clusters.

Although hard to make, a pineapple will add the necessary high focal point to an arrangement. Color several cupsfull of soap clay beige by adding red, green and blue food coloring. Shape the clay into a cone and round the top and bottom. Dent the center of the small end so you can add leaves later.

With a paring knife, criss-cross the entire surface of the cone. Spread yellow and orange food coloring over the crosses with your finger. Add a crown of long, slender, green leaves and hold them straight above the cone until they harden.

Complete your centerpiece by arranging lemons, limes, plums, oranges, apples, bananas, and grapes around your pineapple in a shallow pedestal bowl. Let a few grapes from each cluster dangle over the side of the bowl to give a realistic effect.

Any variety of flowers can be made by cutting the leaves and petals from flattened soap-clay, and attaching them to round clay centers. An arrangement of fruits and flowers makes a lovely spring centerpiece.

Using another form of soap sculpture, you can make a Christmas village of miniature houses, churches, sleighs, and trees; a rabbit or basket of eggs for Easter; boats, valentines, cherry trees, or anything you want. Cut your figures from cardboard and tape them together. Add a little water to detergent and whip it with a rotary beater until it is the consistency of cake frosting.

Tint your mixture with food coloring and spread it over the figures with a spatula. Use heavier pieces of soap-clay for eyes, ears, and other features.

Soap figures make charming gifts because they are decorative, fragrant smelling, and they dissolve in water. When the decorative uses for soap-figures have been exhausted, the "fruits of your labor" have not been in vain, for soap-figures make wonderful bubble bath!

Why should you pay $17.00 for a terrarium when you can make one for under a dollar?

Chapter 17
Beautiful Bottles

Glass is one of the elements that we can all recycle. And, like good citizens, we should return all "for deposit" bottles. Others, we can bring to recycle depository centers. Or, use them in one of hundreds of creative craft projects.

Immediately, when I think of recycling glass bottles, I think of terrariums. Not long ago, the Los Angeles Times Magazine did a full-color, four-page spread in their Home Magazine about my home full of beautiful junk. Featured here was one of my favorite items—an old Baker's rack, stacked with all sizes, colors and shapes of terrariums. The rack was free, from the garbage behind the bakery. Rust removed with vinegar and water, spray painted antique black, it was perfect for my glass garden.

I had seen terrariums in floral and gift shops selling for $12. and up. It seemed to me that anyone could do the same thing for no more than one dollar per bottle. I decided to try it. You'll want to, too.

First, collect large, small, and unique bottles with different colorings and shapes. I think apple cider, wine, vinegar or syrup bottles give the best variety.

From my own experience, plants in terrariums die most often from improper drainage, which causes the roots to rot. Or, because the sun hits the bottle and burns the plants up. So, let's begin with our drainage problem. Make a funnel from paper, and hold it securely in the neck of your bottle. Of course, we're assuming that your bottle has been washed and rinsed, and is ready for planting.

Now, drop small drainage rocks, available in floral shops, into the bottle. Shake gently so the rocks evenly coat the bottom. Put in about an inch of these drainage rocks. This time with planting soil, also available in floral, garden or grocery stores, shake in about two inches of soil through your funnel. Gently shake the bottle to evenly distribute the soil over the rocks.

Some people prefer to water their terrarium after planting. Again, from my own experience, because the soil is very light and porous, I dampen the soil before planting. You may use a large eye-dropper for this. Watch the soil darken as it becomes moist with water. But, do not saturate. It's most important that you remember not to overwater your terrarium.

Planting is not as difficult as you might think. Of course, you may drop seeds into your terrarium—just be certain to use only one or two, and be sure the plants will never grow more than three to five inches high. Another point to remember: Do not overcrowd your terrarium. If you are using seeds, drop through the funnel; gently scoop a light cover of soil over them with a long stick.

If you prefer to plant young plants, may I suggest asparagus fern and one or two varieties of ivy. Make sure all your plants are small and do consider how compatible they are together. For example: Do they all like water, or are there forms of cactus next to ferns? It's best not to mix the two in one terrarium. Incidentally, a cactus terrarium should be made from soil that's at least half sand. Also, make certain that the plants in all your terrariums provide a variety of size and color.

In planting, simply dig a hole in the soil with your long stick. Drop the plant through the neck of the bottle, gently push the plant into the hole, and again, push the soil around the plant with your long stick. Do the same to the next plant . . . until three or four are secure in a large terrarium, maybe only two plants in a smaller one.

I like to add colored rocks or tiny figurines to my terrariums. It helps to create a charming "fairy tale" garden. If you haven't watered your terrarium before planting, do so now.

Set your terrarium where it will receive indirect sunlight; never, never near a window. Believe it or not, now you're through, and you needn't do a thing to your miniature garden again. Your little garden should grow on its own, providing you with an interesting hobby and a lovely decoration.

Sometime in the next six months, check to see if the soil appears a bit dry. If it does, set an ice cube on the bottle's neck. As the ice cube melts, it will provide enough moisture to satisfy the plants.

To think you almost paid $12 for a $1 item! Aren't you glad you went "junkshopping"?

If your interest is not in terrariums, you might turn your bottles into decorative containers. You may stain them with any of the liquid plastic products available in hobby shops. One inexpensive stain is used for painting the backs of glass aquariums. Ask for it at your local pet shop. You brush it on the glass bottle, and it dries, forming crystals like frost. This liquid plastic comes in about ten colors, so you may stripe it, polka-dot it, or use your imagination to do anything you wish.

I'll never forget the day I found a box of clear glass bottles in a local junkshop. They were about five inches high, squarish, stoppered, and very antique looking.

The dealer said they were French perfume bottles, and I could have the whole box for $5. Do you know, I was so excited about these bottles, that dollar signs actually danced before my eyes! I could just imagine the bottles stained and selling for at least twice what I paid for them.

Later, at home, while brushing on the liquid plastic, I saw tiny print on the bottom of one of the bottles. Closer examination revealed that it said, MADE IN JAPAN.

Always save your glass bug bombs at the end of the summer. Striped with liquid plastic, decorated with ribbons and bows, filled with tiny perfumed soaps, they make lovely accessories for the bathroom. You now have a charming, inexpensive gift for a hostess, a club exchange, or for someone who needs a bath.

IT COULDN'T BE DONE

by EDGAR A. GUEST

Somebody said that it couldn't be done,
    But he with a chuckle replied
That "maybe it couldn't," but he would be one
    Who wouldn't say so till he tried.
So he buckled right in with the trace of a grin
    On his face. If he worried he hid it.
He started to sing as he tackled the thing
    That couldn't be done, and he did it.

Somebody scoffed: "Oh, you'll never do that,
    At least no one ever has done it;"
But he took off his coat and he took off his hat,
    And the first thing we knew he'd begun it,
With a lift of his chin and a bit of a grin,
    Without any doubting or quiddit,
He started to sing as he tackled the thing
    That couldn't be done, and he did it.

There are thousands to tell you it cannot be done,
    There are thousands to prophesy failure;
There are thousands to point out to you, one by one,
    The dangers that wait to assail you.
But just buckle in with a bit of a grin,
    Just take off your coat and go to it;
Just start to sing as you tackle the thing
    That "cannot be done," and you'll do it.

TERRIFIC ANY-BOTTLE TERRARIUM

"Recycle" any clear or lightly-tinted glass bottle or jug into a terrarium:

a. Scrub your bottle, removing all labels. Rinse and allow to dry.

Shape an 8 inch by 10 inch paper into a funnel the size of the neck of your bottle, to allow soil to slide into your terrarium. For a gallon jug or bottle, drop in one package Uncle Milton's Planting Mix. Shake gently to spread. If you are using a smaller bottle, use less Basic Plant Mix.

c. Test to see if the patented "Green Thumb" miniature garden tool (in your kit*) will fit through the neck of your bottle. If so, attach "Green Thumb" to a long stick or a coat hanger with a rubberband. If not, use the long, round cardboard portion of a hanger for your gardening tool. With your gardening tool, scratch a hole in the soil. Now it's time for planting.

d. Use any variety of plants, one to three inches high, except cactus. It's nice to combine ivy and ferns in the same terrarium. Carefully drop your first plant into the terrarium. Gently push and straighten your plant with the gardening tool until it is standing upright in the hole you dug. Push soil around it to form a small mound. Follow the same procedure for the second plant, and maybe a third. It is best not to overcrowd your terrarium. Example: A gallon jug can comfortably house three small plants.

e. The first watering of your miniature garden is very important. Too much water will rot the plant's roots. At your sink, turn the cold water tap on to little more than a trickle. Allow just enough water to slip down the inside surface of your jug to clean and water at the same time. Turn, washing all inside surfaces, as quickly as possible. Do not allow too much water to enter your terrarium. It should be moist, but not soaked.

f. Again using your paper funnel, drop decorators' pebbles (from your kit*) into the terrarium for added color. You may also add small statues, bridges, etc. It's not necessary to stopper your bottle or jug, but you may if you wish. Just remember to remove the stopper every two days to allow fresh air to enter.

g. Now your terrarium is almost self-sustaining. Remember that you should never place your terrarium in direct sunlight. The rays, passing through the glass, will burn the plants. And, you need not water the terrarium but once every two months. At that time, four droppers of water is all that is necessary.

*"Sari's Junk Box" is available in toy and hobby departments.

Chapter 18
Build Your Walls of Ivy

In Texas I learned that branding irons make elegant candle holders. Unless you really need them for what they were made for.

124

A clever room divider-planter can be made from an old bookcase or table, three lengths of cylindrical wood, and your ivy houseplants.

Place the end of a small bookcase or table against the wall where the room is to be divided, and measure the distance between the ceiling and the top of the bookcase.

Purchase three pieces of round wood, 1-1/2 inches in diameter, each the length you measured.

Attach these cylindrical poles to the bookcase top in the following way: measure the width of the top and mark the center; measure the length of the top and place a dot at the half-point; mark a dot at each end, each one two inches in from the end. Now, find the three spots for each pole by putting an X in the middle of the width at each of the three spots you marked along the length.

Place a screw on the underside of the bookcase top, below one of the Xs you marked, and turn until a glimmer of the screw's tip can be seen coming through. Hold your pole over it and screw until tight.

When the three poles are in place you can measure the length between the center pole and each end pole to determine the size of the planters you'll need. Build or buy your planters—here you can use your own ingenuity.

Now comes the fun—your chance to be an interior decorator! Paint, stain, or varnish the bookcase, box planters, and poles. A living room divider, stained Walnut, complements Danish Modern furniture; a kitchen or family room divider can be striking if you make the bookcase one color, such as lavender, the planters another color, blue, and each pole a different color, one pale green, one sherbert orange and one powder blue.

When the paint is dry, plant your ivy in the boxes, place them on the bookcase between the poles, and wind the ivy tendrils around the poles toward the ceiling. Attach the tendrils with clear tape or thread.

What fun you'll have creating patterns with your ivy as it grows—wind it back and forth between two poles until you have a solid wall of ivy, tape it to the ceiling between the poles to achieve a tropical effect, or drape it in an artistic shape all your own!

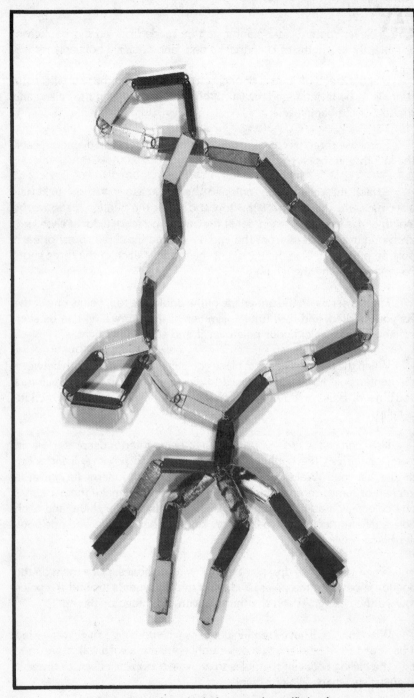

Paper clips and gum-backed paper make terrific jewelry.

Chapter 19
Fashions and Fun with Paper Clips

Like me, over the years you've probably tossed hundreds of paperclips into the waste basket. After all, one paperclip seems terribly insignificant when you're cleaning the house. Yet, the price of metal is so high today that I felt paperclips deserved a second, more creative look.

Of course, paperclips are essential in an office, but did you know that they can be made into window curtains, lovely room dividers, or decorative wall hangings? Not only that, but children love making paperclip jewelry. And, this gives them a chance to create gifts for their friends, and accessories for their own wardrobe. Another clever idea: you can make a lovely rope trim for your Christmas tree from paperclips and scraps of paper. Intrigued? I was, too. So, let me share my discoveries about paperclips with you.

My classes at Carthay Center School are designed to take children, ages five to twelve, junkshopping ecologically. An inventory of miscellaneous, recycleable items at the school and at the children's homes, revealed a good supply of used and new paperclips. So, we bought sticky-backed decorator tape (about 50 cents for a large, 1/2 inch wide role). Since we were between Halloween and Thanksgiving, I selected autumn colors: orange, brown, red and yellow. Incidentally, scraps of gum-backed wallpaper or shelving paper work just as well.

Cut your tape or your paper so you have approximately an inch-wide square. While you're cutting the squares of tape, the children can link paperclips into a long chain. You probably won't have to teach them how to do this! Naturally, if children are making bracelets, their paperclip chain will be less than six inches long. Necklaces can be long or short, but should be long enough to safely slip over the child's head. Now, you and your little ones, wrap the tape or gummed-back paper around the paperclips. The patterns we chose were mostly one orange, one red, one yellow, one brown. Repeat. But some youngsters made five red paperclips, then one yellow, then five red again, or whatever they felt was right. More artistic individuals in my class made a double row of clips to hang around their necks. Others, added a paperclip tassel. Simply attach four to six short strings of paperclips (three or four inches long each) to the end of the necklace. You'll be absolutely amazed at the beauty of paperclip jewelry. Paper wrapped clips actually resemble beads!

Now, mom and dad, are you ready for our large paperclip project? A unique window treatment can be made from shutters and strings of paperclips, or just long strings of paperclips. Equally dramatic are doorways, room dividers and wall hangings made the same way.

Naturally, you should string your clips to the length you desire your window curtains, doorway, room divider or wall hanging to be. Choose the colors you wish to use to compliment your room. Wrap the gummed paper, cut into one-inch squares, around each paperclip, and smooth it down.

When you have completed your chains of paperclips to the proper length, attach them to round, brass cafe curtain loops. These, of course, are available in hardware stores. Slide the loops onto round brass cafe rods. Choose a rod the proper width of your window, doorway or the desired width of your wall hanging. This will enable your chains to slide if you need to walk through them, or to slide if you wish to permit sunlight to come through the curtain.

By now, you've guessed how to make your Christmas tree chain. We made ours about twelve feet long and adorned it with red, green and silver decorator tape. But, also, you could use salvageable pieces of aluminum foil. Since we're not using many electric lights this year, due to the energy crisis, the foil adds a welcome glitter to the tree.

Of course, you can hang little bells or glass balls on your paperclip chain, or anything that captures your imagination.

Another clever idea: We draped one of our paperclip chains over the fireplace mantle. With a stapler, we attached Christmas cards to the chains, and we used this as a decoration and a useful way to display our treasures.

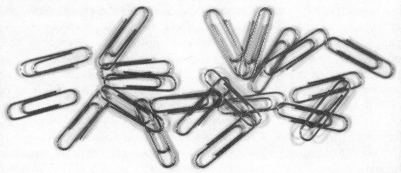

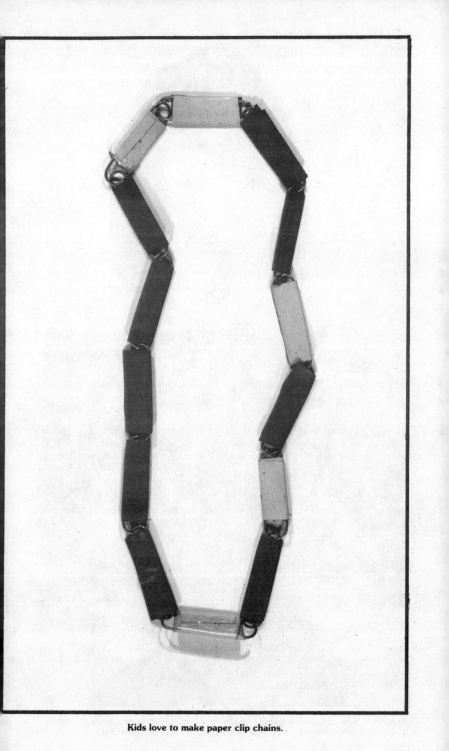

Kids love to make paper clip chains.

Troy holds one of my most popular teaching projects. Simply sew dried or preserved leaves and flowers to cardboard. Frame and spray paint. You have an original.

130

Chapter 20

"The Children Junk-it Themselves

Troy's Headshop by Troy

Hi! My name is Troy. I'm my mom's Number One son, because I'm the oldest. I guess I inherited some of my mom's creative talents because I'm real good at "Junkshopping." For instance, once I was playing with my homemade clay—Make it from about a loaf of white bread with crust torn off. Add half a cup or so of white glue and several teaspoons liquid starch. Knead until the consistency of clay-dough, adding more bread or starch, according to texture desired.

Anyway, I couldn't think what I wanted to make from this clay-dough, and I thought of a Headshop, and how popuar they are. Everybody knows that a Headshop has incense, candles, cards, posters and other gifts. But, I wanted to make my own Headshop, and my crazy imagination told me to make a bunch of heads and arrange them on a miniature shelf. Out of the clay-dough, I made many backgrounds like white heads, black heads, yellow heads, Indian heads, etc.

I painted them all with oil paints, when the dough sculptures had dried. On some, I glued feathers for a headdress. Others, had little hats made of cardboard and scraps of felt. Still others wore cotton hair and beards, or longer hair made from yarn scraps. Beads and sequins added trim, or occasionally, eyes. No two were alike, but all my "heads" were fun.

Now I needed a stand or a shelf to put them on. So, I found a cigar box and I antiqued it with shoe polish. Then, I held it a few inches from a candle's flame. This gave a rustic, older look to my tiny shelf. I hung my "Headshop" with a macrame rope my sister made for me. I was pleased because it was a unique decoration, utilizing three creative ideas. And, boy is my "Headshop" a conversation piece. HaHa.

Troy has a good sense of humor. I bet you already guessed that when you saw his collection of sculpted heads arranged on a cigar box. He calls it "Headshop."

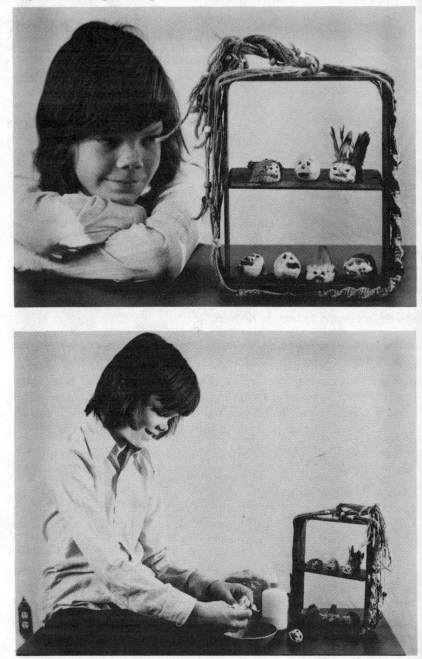

I couldn't find a use for toilet paper rolls. Little Tamma did it with her "toilet paper candle!" And it's cute! .

Toiletpaper Candle
by Tamma

Hello! I'm, Tamma, my mom's second littlest child. I'm nine. I like to "junkshop," too. One day I was thinking what I could do with a toilet-paper roll that I was going to throw away. A great idea came into my head: Maybe I could make a candle out of it? It would be fake, of course, but it would be a great decoration for my room.

I experimented, and after I had made the decoration, it was so cute I thought I'd tell you how to do it. First, I covered the toilet roll with orange paper. Naturally, I glued this down. Make it any color you like. I used a light-weight construction paper. I cut a circle for the top, and taped it in place.

Next, I got a peanut butter jar lid and glued the toilet roll to the up-turned peanut butter lid. Now I cut a slit in the top of the toiletpaper roll, and added a paper candle flame. Then I took several pipecleaners and twisted them together, and formed them into a handle for the candle-holder peanut butter lid.

As a last touch, I arranged greenery around the base of the candle, sitting in the jar lid. You can use pine or jade, or whatever is handy in your yard.

Setting on my dresser, my candle is really cute.

Terra creates necklaces and bracelets from strips of magazines and newspapers. Her friends are begging for the recipe. Here it is.

Beads
for
Terra
by
Terra

My name is Terra. And I am thirteen. I've got some talent, too! I model, dance, and I'm a little bit creative. (Which comes in handy!) Around Christmas, I have friends and relatives galore! So, I make most of my presents.

For a lot of friends, I make necklaces, chokers and bracelets. "Well, who can't do that!" you may ask yourself. But, I make beads out of magazine paper and glue!

First, you cut long triangular strips of paper from an old magazine. Then roll the strips on a pencil, starting from the wider end and ending with the narrowest point in the center. Then just glue the point and pull out the pencil and . . . you have a bead!

Make as many as you would, depending on how long you would like your necklace or item to be. Spray them with shellac, or hair spray, to add a professional touch. You can also string a bell along with the beads, or any decorative piece that would add interest.

Little Michael and his buddy, our collie "Wolf," use paper clips as creative toys.

Mike,
The Mighty Builder
by Mama & Mike

My adorable, chubby, Baby Michael, the two-and-a-half-year old boss of this house, is also a junkshopper. It took this bright, little guy two trips to the thrift shop to learn that that was the place to get "toys."

Of course, used toys are much cheaper, though still just as attractive to a two-year-old, so I can buy more of them. Mike picks out something, hands the change that I give him to the proprietor, and walks to the car clutching his treasure to his chest. He already knows the pride of "making a good deal."

When I felt that Mikie was old enough to enjoy building blocks, the kids and I made him a giant set. Terra, Troy and Tamma helped me to gather round, rectangular and square boxes. In fact, we collected over twenty boxes of all sizes and shapes. Next, we covered them completely with scraps of gum-backed paper. (You can buy odd bits, scraps and remnants at the hardware store for half the price).

As a last touch, we smoothed interesting decals on each side of each block. Some of the decals pictured things that Mikie really likes. Things that he identifies with. Others, such as numbers and letters, were perfect for teaching purposes. In fact, the kids made a game of asking him to tell them what a letter on a block was. He learned it twice as fast because it was on an item he frequently played with.

Again, a few coats of liquid plastic were very helpful in preserving these toys. Also, they can then be washed with a damp cloth.

When Terra was a little younger, she decided that she wanted to add a few "junkshop" items to her bedroom. We went out seeking together, and came back with an adorable old school desk. I left Terra in the garage hosing down our dusty treasure, and went in to start dinner.

Shortly after that, I heard a shriek from the garage. I charged down and joined my daughter . . . an army of tiny black spiders was disembarking from their watery nest. I seemed they'd taken-up lodging in the desk's inkwell for some time!

We painted the desk together, chatting about school and hobbies and fun. When it was a bright yellow, with barn-red wrought iron legs, we brought it into her room. I "planted" a vase of flower-tipped pens and pencils in the tiny inkwell on the desk. Terra still uses these for homework every night. From a kerosene lamp, we made a study lamp for the desk. Since it was now electric, we stored colorful gumdrops in the clear glass base that formerly had held kerosene.

Little Tamma joined in on this hobby, even though she was only five, by helping me to create a puppet theatre. We knocked the back from an old, carved shadowbox. When painted a cheery red, we strung a lace curtain across the back. Most fun of all was in gathering miniature dolls, pictures for the "set," and furnishings. As you can see, we were very fortunate to find a miniature chest and some tiny books.

Now, when Tamma wanted to give a show, she set the shadowbox on a chair, kneeled behind it, and worked her puppets on thick knitting needles. When she tired of Barbie doll puppets, she tried stuffed animals. Whatever, that was just about her favorite toy.

In the girls' room, above their rose-colored bed, we arranged collages of real antique dolls, art awards from school, bric a brac that they had collected at garage sales, or whatever they wanted. To this day, they keep a current collage wall in their bedrooms.

Troy, the artist, we call him, went many steps further in his bedroom. He wanted a worn-out pair of waterskis for shelving on his walls, and I agreed to help him. I mounted pegboard brackets on the wall, attached the pegboard, and hooked the skis to these. That way, if he should change his mind and decide to try something else, he could.

Troy painted the skis blue, mounted them, and arranged his treasures as he liked them. Later, when we found an old life preserver at a garage sale, we turned it into a picture frame, and a mirror at different times.

Troy's unique bedroom shelves were actually made from waterskis which we wore out on skiing trips. Repainted, they make marvelous shelves.

Above the girls' beds are a variety of objects d'arte that they gathered themselves. This, of course, is their "collage wall."

An old school desk, rejuvenated, is a charming and useful addition to Tena's room.

Chapter 21
Thinking Positively

You know, my friends, thinking positively is a great asset! There have been books written on the subject—there have been radio and TV programs, and the written word has told us down through generations—one way or another—that thinking positive is the secret of success. I usually end arguments with people by giving them a printed card that says "procrastination is the secret of failure." So, if you are thinking of making something out of junk and if you have learned a bit about the art of junk shopping, then **do it now.** You don't have to furnish your entire home with renovated junk, but you can start with one or two items that Sari has shown you "How To" in this book. You can either find most of the materials lying around your own house or spend a few pennies and purchase a few of the component parts. Whichever way—get started and get busy! Anyone can create a painting by numbers and anyone can put together a hobby kit by following directions. But the greatest instructions are the ones that are stored in your own mind.

Make something out of junk! We hope that we have taught you how to be a junkie, and we hope that we have given you a few ideas on how to actually refinish, recover or reconstruct a piece of junk, so do it—and do it NOW!

You may even win a prize. Take time to read the next chapter very carefully.

Uncle Milt

Chapter 22
A Prize For Your Possession

GOOD LUCK Sari

Sari, c/o Uncle Milton Industries, Inc.
Dept. HT
10459 West Jefferson Boulevard,
Culver City, California, 90230

"HOW TO BE A JUNKIE" CONTEST

During one of our brain storming sessions, which you read about previously, a member of the panel came up with the idea of offering a prize, or several prizes, to the readers of this book who created either the most beautiful or the most unique item out of junk. Immediately, the rest of the panel objected because it would be quite a task to have a mailman and/or the REA truck unload hundreds and even thousands of pieces of converted items at the factory door. It was finally agreed that the projects would be judged strictly by Sari and that only photographs would be accepted for judging. That is, photographs of the pieces or products that were created by the readers.

So, here's the deal:

1. Create something, but it must be created out of junk.

2. Take a snapshot of it. You don't have to get a professional photographer. You can just send us a small snap or a polaroid shot.

3. Address it to Sari, c/o Uncle Milton Industries, Inc. Dept. HT 10459 West Jefferson Boulevard, Culver City, California, 90230 and mark the outside of the envelope "HOW TO BE A JUNKIE" CONTEST.

4. Since we expect a pretty good volume of letters and photographs, please be patient because it may take a month to six weeks before the prize winners are announced.

5. The prizes will consist of a United States Savings Bond and many other valuable items.

This will be, more or less, a fun contest, and Sari says that she will make judgment on the originality of the products rather than the clarity of the photographs. If you wish, you may accompany the photograph with a 25 word or less description telling us what you bought for your basics and what you did to complete the item. Good luck!

ROUGE

A simple preparation of rouge is made as follows:

Carmine, 1/2 dram
Oil of almonds, 1 dram
French chalk, 2 ounces

Mix thoroughly, and it will be found that the chalk absorbs the oil, making an adhesive powder. One advantage in using this rouge is that it does not contain any mercury.

FACE POWDER

Rice flour, 3 ounces
Rice starch, 3 ounces
Carbonate of magnesia, 1-1/2 ounces
Pulverized boric acid, 3/4 ounce

Powdered orris, 3/4 dram
Essence of citron, 7 drops
Essence of bergamot, 7 drops

Mix the essences with the magnesia, and then combine with the powder. Strain before using.

LIP SALVE

Spermaceti ointment, 1/2 ounce
Balsam of Peru, 7-1/2 grains
Alkanet, 7-1/2 grains
Oil of cloves, 2 drops

Mix the alkanet with the spermaceti ointment, in a bottle or in a dish, and let it stand over a gentle heat til the liquid is rose-colored, then put it through a strainer. When cool, stir in the balsam and let it settle.

When it is clear, pour off the liquid, leaving the sediment, then add the cloves to the liquid. When it becomes cold, it should be hard, but it will not get hard if, in the course of making, it has been subjected to too much heat; therefore, it should simply be allowed to get warm.

CHINESE EYELASH STAIN

Gum arabic, 1 dram
India ink, 1/2 dram
Rose-water, 4 ounces

Powder the ink and gum, and triturate small quantitites of the powder until there is obtained a uniform black liquid in a powder, and then add the rose-water. Be careful not to get this stain in the eyes.

TO DARKEN THE EYEBROWS

Make a strong brew of sage tea, strain it through a muslin, and to a pint of the liquid add a tablespoon of alcohol. Apply this to the eyebrows with a brush. It is perfectly harmless, and will, in fact, stimulate the growth of the eyebrows.

PERFUMED BEADS

Old-fashioned perfumed beads are made in the following manner:
Powdered red-rose petals, 4 ounces
Carmine, 20 grains
Tincture of musk, 1 dram
Gum tragacanth

Mix all the ingredients together, and add enough of the gum tragacanth to mold into spheres; piece them before they are perfectly dry. They can be highly polished, or can be incised in various fashions.

ORANGE-FLOWER CREAM

Oil of sweet almonds, 4 ounces   Glycerin, 1-1/2 ounces
White wax, 6 drams   Oil of neroli, 15 drops
Spermaceti, 6 drams   Oil of orange-skin (bigarde) 15 drops
Borax, 2 drams

Melt the sweet almond, wax, and spermaceti, and add to it the orange-flower water. Dissolve the borax in the mixture, and then pour it slowly into the blended fats, stirring continuously. This is a good "food for the skin."

SCENT-BAGS

An old-fashioned filling for scent-bags is made as follows:

Coriander seed, 1/4 pound   Lavender blossoms, 2 ounces
Powdered orris-root, 1/4 pound   Mace, 1/2 ounce
Aromatic calamus, 1/4 pound   Cinnamon, 14 ounce
Damask-rose leaves, 1/4 pound   Cloves, 1/4 ounce
Powdered musk, 2 drams

Beat each separately, then mix well together.

ROSE SACHET

Dried rose-leaves, 1/2 pound
Ground sandal-wood, 1/4 pound
Attar of rose, 1/8 ounce
Keep in a tightly corked bottle when not needed for use to fill the bags

ATTAR OF ROSE

Rose leaves
Salt
Olive oil

Pick enough rose leaves to make a quart when closely pressed down. Put a layer of these in a 2-quart glass fruit jar, and sprinkle lightly with salt, then cover with a thin layer of absorbent cotton wet with olive oil.

Fill the jar with alternate layers in the same manner, put on the rubber cover and set the jar in the sun daily for 2 weeks, or longer, if the weather be cloudy.

Uncover, and press the oil from the leaves and cotton, and place it in very closely corked vials. Makes a heavenly perfume oil.

FALLING HAIR

Glycerin, 1/2 ounce
Eau de Cologne, 1/4 pint
Liquid ammonia, 1 dram
Oil of rosemary, 1/2 dram
Oil of organum, 1/2 dram
Tincture of cantharides, 1 ounce

Mix and agitate well for 10 minutes. A few drops of essence of musk, or other perfume, may be added if so desired.

EGG SHAMPOO

A good egg shampoo can be easily made as follows:

Egg, 1
Hot rainwater, 1 pint
Spirits of rosemary, 1 ounce

Beat the mixture thoroughly and use it warm. Rub it well into the scalp, and rinse several times in clear water.

POWDER FOR OILY HAIR

A powder to clean oily hair is made as follows:

Powdered orris, 1/4 pound
Bergamot rind, 1-1/3 drams
Cassia flowers, 1-1/2 drams
Coarsely ground cloves, 1/4 drams

Mix all, and put through a sieve. The best way of using is to rub into the hair at night, and let it remain until morning, then brush it out. This will perfume the hair.

TO KEEP THE HAIR CURLED

The following mixture will keep the hair curled:

Gum arabic, 1 ounce

Alcohol, 2 fluid ounces

Moist sugar, 1/2 ounce

Bichlorid of mercury, 6 grains

Hot water, 3/4 pint

Sal-ammoniac, 6 grains

The mercury and sal-ammoniac should be dissolved in the alcohol before mixing with the other ingredients. At the last add enough water to make the whole mixture measure 1 pint. Perfume with cologne or lavender water. Moisten the hair with the fluid before putting it in papers or curlers. This is too strong a solution to be applied repeatedly, as it would surely have a destructive effect on the hair follicles, and for that reason it should not be applied too frequently, nor at too short intervals. An occasional use, however, is practically harmless.

VEGETABLES AS MEDICINE

Asparagus benefits the kidneys.
Potatoes contain salts and potash.
French beans and lentils give iron.
Celery is good for rheumatism and neuralgia.
Tomatoes stimulate the healthy action of the liver.
Lettuce is good for tired nerves, and induces sleep.
Cabbage, cauliflower and spinach are beneficial to anemic people.

Food specialists vote spinach as the most precious of vegetables. It contains salts of potassium and much iron.

It is claimed that carrots form blood, beautify the skin, and improve the appetitie.

For that tired feeling that comes in the spring, the best vegetables are parsley, horseradish, mustard, dock, dandelion and beet-tops, as they clear the blood, and regulate the system.

Gather the rose leaves in the morning and let them stand in a cool place to dry. Toss them lightly, then put them in a large covered dish in layers. Sprinkle each layer freely with salt.

Add to this several mornings, till enough stock of leaves has been gathered. Shake up, or stir every morning, and let the whole stand 10 days after the last petals are added.

Transfer to a glass fruit-jar, in the bottom of which have been placed the allspice and cinnamon. Let it stand 6 weeks closely covered, when it is then ready for the permanent jar.

Add to it now orris, lavender, and a small quantity of any other sweet-scented dried leaves that may be desired, and mix all together, and put it into the permanent rose-jar, in alternate layers; with the rose stock and the few drops of roseoil, pour over the whole a fourth of a pint of good strong cologne.

This will last for years; though from time to time one may add a little lavender, or orange-flower water, or any nice perfume, and at some seasons, may even add a few more fresh rose-petals.

CURE FOR SEASICKNESS

A glass of hot milk with a generous dash of cayenne will often cure seasickness.

SICK HEADACHE

The juice of half a lemon, in a cup of black coffee, without any sugar, has been found to cure a sick headache.

STINGS OF INSECTS

To relieve the stings of insects, apply ammonia or peroxide to the affected part. An old-time cure was as follows:

Take the sting out with a needle and then with the place tightly squeezed, suck, and afterwards apply a liniment of powdered chalk and olive oil to the part.

TO CURE A BILIOUS ATTACK

A strong, unsweetended lemon, taken before breakfast, will prevent and will cure a bilious attack.

TOOTH-POWDER

The following recipe gives an excellent tooth-powder, easily made, and pleasant to use:

Peruvian bark, 1/2 ounce
Myrrh, 1/2 ounce
Powdered Orris-root, 1/2 ounce
Chalk, 1 ounce
Flavor very strongly with wintergreen

We have compiled these recipes for cosmetics, perfumes, health remedies, and cleaning formulas from a collection of antique cookbooks from 80 to 125 years old. We do not recommend any recipe for use . . . though they may work beautifully, we only present them as examples of ancient do-it-yourself chemistry. We do know that all the requested ingredients can still be found at your local drugstore.

Chapter 24
Yummy
Tried and Tested
Antique Recipes

SWEET TOOTH

February is cake-baking month. I learned this from my mother. I can still see her, embraced in a clean print housedress, moving from the mixer to the oven at least twice a week during this month.

As soon as she'd dabbed the last bit of frosting on one cake, (and handed me the mixer beaters and bowls to lick), she'd start another.

What did she do with all the cakes she baked in February? Some went to neighbors for Valentine's Day gifts, others into the freezer to be eaten when unexpected company dropped in. But always one cake snuggled temptingly beneath the big cake pan on the kitchen counter.

My mother permitted raids on that cake pan once a day—when we pounded in from school. How breathless we were, having run all the way, knowing that treat lay ahead of us!

More often than not, the cake beneath that pan was made with pure honey. (Mom's antique secret for cakes that remained moist up to a week). Frequently they were chocolate (dad's favorite). People often marveled at the chocolatey flavor of mother's cakes. She shared her secret with me only after I had been married two years.

"Add a pinch of salt and a dash of vanilla to bring out the goodness in chocolate," she said, "and always undercook chocolate cakes five to 10 minutes.

I loved her honey cake so much that she finally named it after me. Here is her recipe. You may have seen a similar one, but not this exact antique version.

HONEY CAKE

Beat 3 eggs until yellow. Slowly add 1/2 cup sugar. Gently add 1-1/2 cups honey and 1 cup oil. Beat well. Add 1 teaspoon vanilla.

Mix and sift 3 times 3 cups flour, 2 teaspoons baking powder, 1 teaspoon baking soda, 1/2 teaspoon salt, scant teaspoon each, cloves, cardamom, allspice, nutmeg, cinnamon and ginger. Add flour mixture to egg mixture, beating continuously, alternately with 1 cup cold coffee, in thirds, ending with flour.

Mix in 1 cup ground nuts, 1/2 cup raisins and 1 tablespoon grated lemon rind. Grease and line 9 x 13 inch pan with waxed paper. Then grease again and lightly flour. Pour batter into pans and bake in preheated 300 degree oven for 1 hour, 10 minutes. Cool on cake rack. Remove from pan when cool and drizzle with "Mama's Honey Frosting."

Combine 1/2 cup honey, 3/4 cup sugar, 1/3 cup milk, 1/4 cup butter and 1/2 teaspoon salt in saucepan. Bring slowly to full rolling boil, stirring constantly. Boil 1 minute. Beat until lukewarm. Add 1 teaspoon vanilla. Beat until right consistency to spread, or drizzle over cake.

When my dad got home from work, the first thing he'd do, (after bidding us kids hello and giving mom a kiss on the cheek), would be to walk over to that cakepan, lift the lid gingerly, and smile if it was chocolate. If it was anything else, he'd politely say, "This looks good, mom."

The chocolate cake dad liked best is 80 years old: CHOCOLATE NOUGAT CAKE.

Sift 1-1/2 cups flour, 2-1/2 teaspoons baking powder, 1 teaspoon salt, and 1-1/2 cups sugar three times. Add 1/3 cup vegetable shortening and 1 cup skimmed milk. Beat at medium speed on an electric mixer for 2 minutes.

Add 2 eggs, 2-1/2 squares unsweetened chocolate (melted), and 1/2 teaspoon red food coloring. Beat 2 more minutes. Add and blend in 1 teaspoon vanilla and 2/3 cup chopped nuts.

Pour batter into two greased and floured 8-inch cake pans. Bake 30 minutes in oven preheated to 350 degrees. Cool on cake rack and frost with your favorite chocolate frosting.

Trying to follow in mom's best cake-baking tradition, three years ago I found a cake recipe in an antique cookbook and redesigned it specifically for Valentine's Day. Since then it has won $15-$50 awards in baking contests.

CUPID'S CLOUD CAKE

Sift 2 cups plus 2 tablespoons flour, 1-1/2 cups sugar, 3-1/2 teaspoons baking powder, and 1 teaspoon salt three times.

Add 1/2 cup soft butter, 1/2 cup milk, 1/2 cup pineapple juice, and 3 teaspoons maraschino cherry juice. Beat 2 minutes at medium speed on electric mixer. (Scrape sides and bottom of bowl constantly.)

Add 4 unbeaten egg whites and beat 2 more minutes. Blend in gently 1 cup crushed, drained pineapple and 10 maraschino cherries cut into small pieces.

Pour into well greased and lightly floured 8 inch layer pans. Bake 35 minutes or until cake tests done with toothpick and gentle push with finger. (If cake springs back after gentle push, it's ready.)

Cool on cake rack and frost with **"Heavenly Pink Frosting."**

Combine 2 unbeaten egg whites, 1-1/2 cups sugar, dash of salt, 1/3 cup water, and 2 teaspoons light corn syrup in top of double boiler.

Beat at high speed on electric mixer for 1 minute. Cook over rapidly boiling water, beating constantly, for 7 minutes. (Frosting will stand in stiff peaks.)

Remove from boiling water and add 1/2 teaspoon vanilla extract and 1/4 teaspoon almond extract. Spread on cake. Sprinkle cake with 1 cup shredded coconut. Place 5 whole pineapple slices in a circle on cake top. Place 5 whole maraschino cherries in the center of each pineapple slice. Serve with pride.

SOUTHERN JAUNT

From Illinois, you can be in Florida in four hours if you fly. But, you miss the delightful and educational experience of sampling native foods in our southern United States. Driving down Route 41 may take you 48 more hours to get there, but you will see homemade candies and a variety of ciders sold in Kentucky; mountain apples in the Tennessee Smokies; famous Georgia peaches and pecans in wayside stands, and Florida orange groves that stretch as far as the eye can see. Mouth watering?

Wait until you sample the traditional recipes my southern relatives passed on to me.

A typical menu in Kentucky will feature "Plantation Beef Stew" and "Hot Biscuits." Prepare the stew with 1-1/2 pounds beef cut in 1-1/2 inch cubes. Boil, covered, for 1-1/2 hours and add 1 cup diced potatoes. Cook for 1 hour until potatoes become mushy.

Add 1/2 cup diced onion, 6 green onions, chopped fine, 1 clove garlic, 1/4 teaspoon black pepper, 1-1/2 teaspoons salt and 1 cup canned green peas. Cook 20 to 25 minutes and serve over hot biscuits that have been split in half.

HOT BISCUITS

Combine 2 cups flour with 5 teaspoons baking powder and 1 teaspoon salt. Add 2 teaspoons shortening and blend until crumbly. Add 1 cup milk and mix until thoroughly blended. Bake in a 450 degree oven for 10 minutes.

Southern biscuits, like hominy grits, are served at every meal and sometimes in between—but always with plenty of butter and honey. In central Florida they are served with orange-blossom honey.

Long before lunchtime in Tennessee, your tummy will growl because the smell of real hickory-smoked pit barbecue haunts the highway like a friendly ghost. "Southern Barbecued Spareribs" are quick and easy fixed this way.

Cut 2 pounds pork spareribs into serving pieces. Place in baking dish and slice 1 medium-size onion over the top. Add 1/4 cup catsup, 1/2 cup water, 1 teaspoon sugar, 1 teaspoon Worcestershire sauce, a dash of Tabasco, and 1/8 teaspoon chili powder. Cover and cook in 350 degree oven for 2 hours.

Once into the Smoky Mountains where cold lakes are stocked with catfish, you will want to try a plate of "Fried Catfish" and "Hush Puppies." Dip cleaned, skinned catfish in beaten egg yolk and then in corn meal that has been seasoned with salt. Fry in large metal skillet containing about 1/4 inch of shortening. When catfish are golden brown and tender to the touch of a fork, serve on a hot platter with coleslaw and "Hush Puppies."

Though there are many ways to make "Hush Puppies," the best recipe I've found is made with 1 cup cornmeal mixed with 1 teaspoon melted butter, 1 teaspoon salt, 1 cup sour milk, 1 teaspoon sugar, 1 egg and 2 teaspoons water. Cook for 20 minutes in the top of a double boiler. Mix 1/2 teaspoon soda with 1 teaspoon water and 1 beaten egg. Add egg mixture to cornmeal mixture when cool. Bake in 400 degree oven for 30 minutes.

The Peach State, Georgia, is also famous for its pecans. "Southern Pecan Pie" is plentiful all along the route. The addition of a meringue topping to this pecan pie recipe makes it even better.

Cream 1/2 cup butter and 1/2 cup sugar together until light and fluffy. Add 3 beaten eggs, 1/2 cup milk, 1 cup corn syrup, 1 cup finely-chopped pecans and 1 teaspoon vanilla. Mix thoroughly and turn into an unbaked pie shell. Bake at 350 degrees for 45 minutes.

When cool, cover with meringue made of 4 egg whites and 8 tablespoons sugar. Do not brown the meringue. Decorate with halves of pecans.

Once in Florida, you can try a piece of the most delicious dessert in the world—"Lime Pie." Make it by blending 1 cup sugar, 3 tablespoons cornstarch, and 1/2 teaspoon salt together. Stir in 1-1/2 cups water and cook until thick. Just before removing from stove, add 2 beaten egg yolks, the juice and 2 teaspoons grated rind from 1-1/2 limes, and 2 tablespoons butter. Cook for five minutes and pour into baked pastry shell. Cover with meringue made from 2 egg whites and 4 tablespoons sugar.

Brown in 325 degree oven. (This recipe may be used with 1 orange (juice and pulp) or 1 lemon (juice and grated rind) instead of lime.

Summertime Menu

From coastal California to the inland sun-baked prairies of Illinois, people were perspiring away their appetites beneath a blow-torch sun. It's my experience that an overheated appetite can easily be stimulated with chilled soups, cold fruit or vegetable salads, and simple, lightly-seasoned meats. Discovered in an antique cookbook, with the delightful memories of California-style eatin' in mind, **"Guacamole Bean Salad"** offers a perfect blend of cool blandness with just enough zest to lift any meal from the dumps.

Chill a 1 pound-12 ounce can of peeled whole tomatoes and a 15-ounce can cut green beans for about three days. Ladle tomatoes from can carefully, draining all liquid possible into the soup kettle. Arrange tomatoes in a deep serving dish; add drained green beans and 1 finely-chopped medium-size onion. Sprinkle temptingly with 3/4 teaspoon Tabasco, 1 teaspoon salt, 1/4 teaspoon freshly ground black pepper, and either a teaspoon of lemon juice or vinegar—(preferably the nourishing apple cider vinegar.)

Mix seasonings, beans, onion and tomatoes very gently, just until blended. Place in refrigerator and allow to mellow for at least three hours before serving.

Present **"Guacamole Bean Salad"** on crisp beds of lettuce in wooden salad bowls, on rounds of buttered toast, or in a soup tureen with a large ladle so every man can serve himself.

The perfect accompaniment, with or beneath **"Guacamole Bean Salad"** is cold roast beef. Slice eight or ten 1/4-inch-thick pieces of left-over beef and fry in 2 tablespoons butter for two minutes on each side. Arrange on platter with slices of swiss cheese, toasted sesame-seed buns, and sweet cherry peppers.

I NEVER WANT TO SEE ANOTHER ARTICHOKE

"What do you do with an artichoke?" my husband asked when I returned from the market bearing two of these lime-green, thick-petaled vegetables that resemble a tropical flower.

"Looks to me like they belong on the rear-section of some prehistoric monster, or in the hands of an angry caveman," he added helpfully.

I merely mumbled something about their being a delicacy that you dipped in melted butter, and that they had been on sale . . . so I thought we'd try them. Too, I thought it about time for me to tackle the ancient art of cooking artichokes.

So, early Saturday morning, when dad had hauled our two-year-old to the barbershop, I unpacked my precious antique foreign cookbooks. Knowing that the French have long held the title for being artistic artichoke eaters, I leafed through the many recipes under A.

Studying the fifteen or so recipes suggested, including "Artichauts au jus," "Fonds d' artichauts," and that grand old favorite, "Il n'y a pas de Petites e' Conomies" . . . I found none that contained more than five ingredients and only one (otherwise rather drab little suggestion) that included fine French wine. This was not the creative French cooking I sought to cultivate. It just wasn't sophisticated enough.

So, I called a worldly wife-mother-artist girlfriend who had spent two years hiking, cycling and artichoking her way about Europe. Sure enough, she had one **real** antique French artichoke recipe containing fine dry white wine and at least ten ingredients, and it was economical, too boot. Here, for all you who have always wondered, is "what to do with an artichoke."

MARINATED ARTICHOKE HEARTS (also ARTICHOKE HASH)

2	medium-sized, firm artichokes
2	garlic cloves, peeled and pressed
1	onion, peeled and sliced in rings
2	slices lemon
2	whole cloves
1-1/3	cups olive oil
1	cup dry white wine (or apple cider vinegar)
1	teaspoon sugar
2	teaspoons salt
1/2	teaspoon dry mustard
6	strips pimento

Wash artichokes and trim off about 1 inch of the stems. Plunge them, stem-end down, into rapidly boiling salted water. Boil for 45 minutes, or until the outer leaves can be easily detached. Drain.

Remove outer leaves. Hold each by the tip, and with a paring knife scrape off the meat from the spiny portion. (Use all these soft, tasty scrapings mixed with butter, ARTICHOKE HASH, as a vegetable at the evening meal.) Discard the spiny portions of the leaves.

Place the chokes, bottoms and stems (the tender portions without spiny leaves), in a 1 quart container with a tight lid, such as a Mason jar. Combine the remaining ten ingredients in jar. Shake gently to mix. Allow to marinate in refrigerator, tightly closed, for several days before serving.

Serve MARINATED ARTICHOKE HEARTS sliced in 1-inch portions on a platter of lettuce as hors-d'oeuvres. Use the marinade as a delicious salad dressing!

Note: If you want to do something else with an artichoke, utilize those spiny leaves you discarded as compost in your Spring garden!

ST. PATRICK'S DAY

The month of the Irish comes around every year. And sure and begora, there will be "little people" leaping about my kitchen, lifting the lid from the iron pot simmerin' on the stove, and shaking their heads unhappily. "Why is it," one small green-clothed fellow once asked me, "that people just don't know how to cook a real old-fashioned **Irish Stew** anymore?"

And so it was that I promised the little feller I'd print his own authentic recipe for Irish Stew in my new book.

IRISH STEW

Brown 2-1/2 pounds cubed round steak with 3 medium-size sliced onions in 3 tablespoons bacon drippings in a large, heavy dutch oven or heavy pot.

Add 1 bay leaf, 4 teaspoons salt, 3 teaspoons caraway seed and 2 cups hot water mixed with 1 cup dry red wine. (Make it 3 cups of water if you wish to omit the wine.)

Cover and cook slowly for 2 hours. Add 1/4 cup vinegar and 1 medium size head of red cabbage cut in wedges; 3 medium-size carrots cut thinly, 2 tablespoons parsley, 2 tablespoons chopped celery and 1 cup thinly-sliced Irish potatoes.

Cover and cook 45 minutes to 1 hour. Remove meat and vegetables from iron pot with a slotted soup ladle; arrange on a hot serving platter.

Add 1 cup crushed gingersnaps to the liquid in the pot, stir until you have a smooth gravy and pour over the hot meat.

(Be certain to garnish your stew with green parsley—in honor of the little fellow who so kindly gave us this recipe.)

It was my husband's mother, whose own mother came directly from Dublin, who gave me the recipes for **"Potato Flour Muffins"** served with **"Rosy Marjoram Jelly."**

POTATO FLOUR MUFFINS

Beat 4 egg whites until very stiff and dry. Add 1/4 teaspoon salt and 1 tablespoon sugar to 4 beaten egg yolks. Fold into the egg whites.

Sift 1/2 cup white potato flour and 1 teaspoon baking powder twice, and thoroughly beat into egg mixture.

Add 2 teaspoons ice water and stir until blended. Pour batter into greased muffin tins and bake in 375 degree oven for 20 minutes.

ROSY MARJORAM JELLY

Pour 1 cup water into a saucepan and bring to a boil. Add 2 tablespoons fresh marjoram leaves, reduce heat, cover and allow to steep 30 minutes.

Strain through double cheesecloth which has been rinsed in cold water and wrung dry. Return pan to heat, add 1/2 cup lemon juice and 3 cups sugar. Stir until dissolved.

Bring to a boil and add 1/2 cup liquid pectin, boiling about 30 seconds. Remove from heat, skim, pour into sterilized jars and seal. Makes 4 cups of delicious jelly to serve with muffins, eggs, cheese and meats.

RICE — A FINE TRADITION

Boiled, baked, fried or steamed, rice is the most important food in all the world. For generations man has depended on rice for his principal food. To some, it represents 70 to 80 per cent of the entire calorie intake.

Here in America, however, rice is traditionally used as a "foundation garment" for a fine meal. Many new cooks, and often learned connoisseurs, are baffled by the various names given to rice recipes. A simple key is to remember that rice is called Pilau in the Near Eastern countries and in some parts of the U.S. Again, in certain parts of the world it is called Pilas. Risotto is rice in Italy; Paella refers to the saffron rice in Spain. These are the noms de plume most often used, but each means rice, flavored and cooked according to the custom of the country.

An antique French rice recipe, borrowed originally from the Italians, and becoming more popular in the U.S., is "Milanaise Risotto."

Fry one finely-chopped onion in butter until it is yellow. Add 1-1/2 cups rice and stir gently until the rice is transparent. Gradually add 6 cups chicken stock, 1 cup at a time, and as the rice absorbs the stock, add more. Sprinkle in a large pinch of saffron. Cook the rice for 30 minutes. It should not be pasty but not completely dry. Sprinkle with 1/4 cup grated Parmesan cheese, season with salt and pepper to taste.

"Saffron Paella," a well-known Spanish recipe, is a delicate operation for any cook. Nevertheless, once you accomplish its intricacy, you'll want to make it a specialty on your family table.

Heat 2 tablespoons olive oil and 2 tablespoons butter in a heavy skillet which has a tight-fitting lid. Add 2 tablespoons finely-chopped onion, 1 clove minced garlic, 1 bay leaf, 1 teaspoon thyme, 1/8 teaspoon rosemary, 1/2 teaspoon salt, 1/4 teaspoon freshly ground black pepper, 1/8 teaspoon cayenne and 1-1/4 cups long grain white rice. Cook over medium heat until rice is a light golden color. (In some parts of Spain the rice is cooked to a deep rich brown.)

Add 1-1/4 cups chicken broth and stir until contents of the skillet are thoroughly mixed. Cover tightly and simmer over low heat until liquid is absorbed and rice tender, about 25 minutes. Add 1/2 to 1 teaspoon saffron to the skillet and serve hot.

A popular Thanksgiving meal accompaniment, "Herbed Wild Rice," originated in France but has long been a favorite of American cooks. Many restaurants feature this recipe with pheasant, turkey or wild duck.

Wash 1 cup wild rice in cold water, changing the water until it becomes clear. Drain and cover rice with 3 cups of cold water, to which 1 teaspoon salt has been added. Place over high heat and bring to a boil but do not stir. Lower heat sufficiently to keep it bubbling until tender, 15 to 40 minutes, depending on rice. Prevent sticking by shaking the kettle now and then, but do not cover and do not stir. When tender, drain and sprinkle with 1 teaspoon finely chopped fresh parsley, 1 teaspoon grated onion, and 1/2 teaspoon basil.

Place in buttered ovenproof serving dish, dot with lumps of butter and place in the oven, tightly covered, at 375 degrees for 15 minutes.

The ability to please those you love with a delicious meal is important in a world filled with insecurities. The art of preparing a good-tasting meal and serving it with elegance should not be confined to the past. Long have French, Italian and German women been known as good cooks. More recently American women have raised their standards of cuisine to encompass foods of all nationalities and their all-American favorites. To every woman who enjoys creating a fine meal three times a day, we tip our hats!

> "That is your poem—too tenuous for a book;
> You are a very gentle perfect cook."
> Walter Lowenfels

PSYCHO-CYBERNETICS
A New Technique for Using Your Subconscious Power
by Maxwell Maltz, M.D., F.I.C.S.

Contents:
1. The Self Image: Your Key to a Better Life 2. Discovering the Success Mechanism Within You 3. Imagination—The First Key to Your Success Mechanism 4. Dehypnotize Yourself from False Beliefs 5. How to Utilize the Power of Rational Thinking 6. Relax and Let Your Success Mechanism Work for You 7. You Can Acquire the Habit of Happiness 8. Ingredients of the Success-Type Personality and How to Acquire Them 9. The Failure Mechanism: How to Make It Work For You Instead of Against You 10. How to Remove Emotional Scars, or How to Give Yourself an Emotional Face Lift 11. How to Unlock Your Real Personality 12. Do-It-Yourself Tranquilizers That Bring Peace of Mind 13. How to Turn a Crisis into a Creative Opportunity.   **268 Pages . . . $2**

A PRACTICAL GUIDE TO SELF-HYPNOSIS
by Melvin Powers

Contents:
1. What You Should Know About Self-Hypnosis 2. What About the Dangers of Hypnosis? 3. Is Hypnosis the Answer? 4. How Does Self-Hypnosis Work? 5. How to Arouse Yourself From the Self-Hypnotic State 6. How to Attain Self-Hypnosis 7. Deepening the Self-Hypnotic State 8. What You Should Know About Becoming an Excellent Subject 9. Techniques for Reaching the Somnambulistic State. 10. A New Approach to Self-Hypnosis When All Else Fails 11. Psychological Aids and Their Function 12. The Nature of Hypnosis   **120 Pages . . . $2**

A GUIDE TO RATIONAL LIVING
by Albert Ellis, Ph.D. & Robert A. Harper, Ph.D.

Contents:
1. How Far Can You Go With Self-Analysis? 2. You Feel as You Think 3. Feeling Well by Thinking Straight 4. What Your Feelings Really Are 5. Thinking Yourself Out of Emotional Disturbances 6. Recognizing and Attacking Neurotic Behavior 7. Overcoming the Influences of the Past 8. How Reasonable is Reason? 9. The Art of Never Being Desperately Unhappy 10. Tackling Dire Needs for Approval 11. Eradicating Dire Fears of Failure 12. How to Stop Blaming and Start Living 13. How to Be Happy Though Frustrated 14. Controlling Your Own Destiny 15. Conquering Anxiety 16. Conquering Self-discipline 17. Rewriting Your Personal History 18. Accepting Reality 19. Overcoming Inertia and Becoming Creatively Absorbed   **208 Pages . . . $2**

A GUIDE TO SUCCESSFUL MARRIAGE
by Albert Ellis, Ph.D. & Robert A. Harper, Ph.D.

Contents:
1. Modern Marriage: Hotbed of Neurosis 2. Factors Causing Marital Disturbance 3. Gauging Marital Compatibility 4. Problem Solving in Marriage 5. Can We Be Intelligent About Marriage? 6. Love or Infatuation? 7. To Marry or Not to Marry 8. Sexual Preparation for Marriage 9. Impotence in the Male 10. Frigidity in the Female 11. Sex "Excess" 12. Controlling Sex Impulses 13. Nonmonogamous Desires 14. Communication in Marriage 15. Children 16. In-laws 17. Marital Incompatibility Versus Neurosis 18. Divorce 19. Succeeding in Marriage 20. Selected Readings   **304 Pages . . . $2**

HOW YOU CAN HAVE CONFIDENCE & POWER
by Les Giblin

Contents:
1. Your Key to Success and Happiness 2. How to Use the Basic Secret for Influencing Others 3. How to Cash in on Your Hidden Assets 4. How to Control the Actions & Attitudes of Others 5. How You Can Create a Good Impression on Other People 6. Techniques for Making & Keeping Friends 7. How to Use Three Big Secrets for Attracting People 8. How to Make the Other Person Feel Friendly—Instantly 9. How You Can Develop Skill in Using Words 10. The Technique of "White Magic" 11. How to Get Others to See Things Your Way—Quickly 12. A Simple, Effective Plan of Action That Will Bring You Success and Happiness.   **180 Pages . . . $2**

The books listed above can be obtained from your book dealer or directly from Melvin Powers. When ordering, please remit 25c per book postage & handling. Send one dollar for our 224 page illustrated catalog of self-improvement books.

Melvin Powers
12015 Sherman Road, No. Hollywood, California 91605